Alberta, Aberhart, and Social Credit

Joseph A. Boudreau

Canadian History Through the Press Series

General Editors:

David P. Gagan and Anthony W. Rasporich

Holt, Rinehart and Winston of Canada, Limited
Toronto : Montreal

Joseph A. Boudreau is Associate Professor of History at California State University, San José, California.

Anthony W. Rasporich, general editor of the *Canadian History Through the Press Series*, is currently Associate Professor of History at the University of Calgary, Alberta.

David P. Gagan, general editor of the *Canadian History Through the Press Series,* is Associate Professor of History at McMaster University, Hamilton, Ontario.

Editors' Preface

Newspapers are widely accepted by historians as useful vehicles of contemporary opinion. In a nation such as Canada, historically dependent on books and periodicals imported from Great Britain and the United States as the principal disseminators of informed opinion, the local daily or weekly newspaper has been almost the sole medium of information and attitudes. And the proliferation of Canadian newspapers since the early decades of the nineteenth century has created for students of Canadian history a vast reservoir of opinion reflecting the political, social, cultural, linguistic, religious and sectional diversity of our country. The *Canadian History Through the Press Series* is an attempt to tap this reservoir by reproducing a cross section of journalistic opinion on major issues, events and problems of the Canadian past.

Using the press as a vehicle for the study of history has already been done with some success in the French series, *Kiosk*, which examines public issues and popular culture in volumes ranging from the Dreyfus affair to French cinema. *Canadian History Through the Press* is not quite so ambitious a venture; but it does aim to introduce the student to events which were compelling subjects of discussion for Canadians through the medium in which public discussion most frequently took place. At its best, the Canadian press is a rich source of historical controversy, providing the historian with a sense of the excitement and contentiousness of contemporary issues. Newspaper editors like William Lyon Mackenzie, George Brown, Henri Bourassa and George McCullagh were themselves often at the centre of the political stage or were, like J.W. Dafoe of the Winnipeg *Free Press,* Joseph Atkinson of the Toronto *Star* and Gérard Pelletier of *La Presse* pundits whose voices were carefully heeded by national and local politicians. This is merely one example of the power of the press; but whatever the subject—Confederation, the Quiet Revolution, social reform, foreign policy or pollution—the press has operated (in Marshall McLuhan's words) as a "corporate or collective image [that] demands deep participation."

As editors of *Canadian History Through the Press* we are committed to the idea that students should be introduced to the study of Canadian history through contemporary documents from the very outset. The newspaper is a familiar, and therefore comfortable, medium for the novice historian. We have chosen to use it exclusively, fully aware of the limitations of the press as an historical source. When a prominent Canadian politician observed recently that his colleagues spent much of their time "quoting yesterday's newspaper" he was acknowledging the power of the press not merely to reflect, but to dictate opinion. And Will Rogers' caricature of the man who "only knew what he read in the paper" is an equally cogent reminder that newspapers should not be used exclusively as a weathercock of opinion. The student, then, must and inevitably will come to grips with both the limitations and the advantages of newspapers as sources of history. In this respect, our series is also aimed at introducing the student to one of the historian's most crucial problems, that of discriminating between conflicting accounts and interpretations of historical events.

The volumes currently published in the *Canadian History Through the Press Series* embrace topics ranging from the War of 1812 to Imperialism and Canada, from economic history to religious issues. It is hoped that this variety of subject matter will permit us to sample not merely the thrust, but the quality of Canadian life.

David P. Gagan,
Anthony W. Rasporich.

Author's Preface

The format of this series has provided me with a unique opportunity to present another viewpoint of a subject that has produced more studies from a variety of approaches than any other political movement in Canadian history. This book is unique, however, in that it allows students of the times and the movement to view the phenomenon as the newspaper readers of the times did; to follow the developments through the news articles; and to evaluate the editorial viewpoints of the press — the generally hostile working press on the one hand, and the laudatory propaganda machinery of the Social Credit movement on the other, together with those newspapers which fell between the two extremes.

In preparing this work I am indebted to the general editors, to Mrs. Margaret Atkins of the San José State University Inter-Library Loan Section, Ms. Jennifer Fullen of the Edmonton Public Library, Miss Sheilagh Jameson of the Glenbow Foundation Archives-Library, Mrs. E. Kreisel of the Alberta Provincial Archives, Mr. Eric Holmgren of the Alberta Provincial Library, Mr. David Elliott of the University of Calgary, Mr. Hugh MacLeod of Mount Royal College, Ms. Doreen Farr who did most of the typing and, most of all, all of my friends and colleagues at the University of Calgary from whom I learned much during my years there from 1962 to 1966.

J. Boudreau,
San José.

Contents

Introduction

I

Albertans frequently complain that their province's role in Canadian history has too often been minimized, misunderstood, or subjected to ridicule and caricature. In particular, because the Social Credit party's years of power (1935-1971) span more than half of the province's modern history, the movement's peculiar reputation outside of Alberta often seems to influence unduly assessments of Alberta's brief history. Grossly stereotyped and underdeveloped, the modern history of the province seems as unbalanced as its earlier experience becomes when it is distorted by simplistic images of mounties, cattle barons, Indians, and railroads. Nevertheless, the fact of Social Credit's phenomenal record remains, and indeed has already served as a stimulant for some of the most interesting scholarship in Canadian historiography. The purpose of this volume is neither to review what has already been said about Social Credit, nor to add to the debate over the movement's meaning and importance in Canadian history. Rather, the documents which follow are intended to convey something of the range and intensity of the debate that went on among Albertans themselves as the Social Credit movement made its appearance, successfully bid for power, then underwent the metamorphosis which allowed it to retain power for thirty-six years, virtually unchallenged.

What was the Social Credit movement? How did it come to power? Why did the Social Credit government of Alberta fail to implement the doctrines which launched the movement and its leader, William Aberhart, on the road to power? These are questions that have been answered in various ways from 1934 down to the present. By reading, as Albertans did, the debates that were carried on through the pages of the local press over these issues, it is possible to revive, follow, and clarify the course of events and the clashes of opinion which marked the evolution of Social Credit from a protest movement into one of the most successful political enterprises in Canadian history. The press, needless to say, was thoroughly biased on one side or the other, and sought to lead public opinion either toward or away from the Social Credit fold depending on the politics of publishers and editors. But if the daily and weekly press attempted to influence public attitudes, it is certain that

1

the newspapers also reflected divisions in local opinion, all the more because Alberta, with its small population divided among two major cities, a dozen small towns and their agrarian hinterlands, in spite of its geographical size was still a narrow and relatively self-contained community whose pulse could be monitored effectively by the local press. The documents, in short, represent Albertans speaking to and for each other.

Before coming to the documents themselves, however, some background to the Social Credit movement in Alberta seems necessary. C.B. Macpherson provides a useful starting point with his concept of Alberta as, historically, a "quasi-colonial" society.[1] Macpherson has argued that the West was primarily the creation of eastern interests, protected by a national tariff policy, dependent on the railroads, the weakest link in the east-west chain of economic interdependence that was the goal of Central Canadian developers and politicians in the late nineteenth century. The term "quasi-colonial" applies to this region because the western farmers, although they were an integral part of the national economic system, were never numerous or powerful enough politically to influence national economic policies for the protection of their own interests. Like other independent but small businessmen, including the merchants and other small commodity producers in the cities and towns of the prairies, they were merely the objects of economic policies devised in the "national" interest, and therefore in the interests of the industrial heartland of Canada.

Largely as the result of this political and economic colonialism, the political tradition of the prairie provinces by the twentieth century was increasingly dominated by the appearance of groups whose principal purpose in life was to badger the national government and the major parties for reforms which took cognizance of the special economic interests of farmers. Moreover, these groups quickly learned that they could not afford to be bound exclusively to either the Liberals or Conservatives given the shifting sands of federal politics and the farmers' perennial need to barter support for promises. Thus, even before 1905, the politicians of the North-West had developed a nonpartisan tradition quite unlike the bipartisan tradition that had emerged in Central Canada early in the nineteenth century. It is true that the creation of the two provinces of Saskatchewan and Alberta in 1905 by Sir Wilfrid Laurier aided Liberal fortunes in the West in the short run, as did Laurier's support for the prairies' favoured economic policy, free trade with the United States, in 1910. But the return of the Conservatives to power in

1911, and the wartime merger of proconscriptionist Liberals with governing Conservatives in Sir Robert Borden's Union government, which refused to modify Conservative tariff policies and insisted on conscripting farmers' sons, again tended to isolate the West from national politics and to discredit regional spokesmen for the two older parties. After the war and the depression which followed it, rural discontent manifested itself nationally in 1921 with the election of sixty-four members of the dissenting National Progressive Party to the House of Commons. In Alberta, in the same year, the local counterpart of the Progressive Party, the United Farmers of Alberta, came to power in Edmonton.

The leader of the United Farmers of Alberta, Missouri-born Henry Wise Wood, advocated his own unique theory of "group government". Wood advanced the idea of government not by party, but rather by economic interest groups who would use the parliamentary process to compromise collectively their conflicting differences in order to provide equitable solutions to the problems of society. Since farmers dominated the society and economy of Alberta, it followed that the farmers' union, the United Farmers of Alberta, embodied their collective interests and hence the interests of most Albertans. Translated into political action, the U.F.A.'s local chapters became political constituency organizations, and its annual meetings political policy conventions.

Each level of deliberation approximated in its own sphere the role of a caucus, the legislature, and the cabinet in the parliamentary system, and indeed improved upon the system by injecting it with a dose of nonpartisan direct democracy, and therefore Wood and his followers had little difficulty equating government in Alberta with the United Farmers' organization, and convincing the majority of Albertans to make the same equation. The United Farmers' government would endure from 1921 until it was replaced in 1935 by Social Credit.

When the Great Depression struck Alberta after 1929, as all of the statistics show, the massive decline in world prices for commodities in general and for farm produce in particular, especially wheat, severely effected the province. All parts of the economy suffered as economic conditions worsened, and the disastrous dust-bowl ecology of the midthirties made a bad situation worse. Generally, it is true, Alberta's agricultural economy was more diversified than Saskatchewan's, and the province was not wholly reliant on wheat for its prosperity. But, as the last part of the West to be settled, Alberta had some special problems of her own. The burdens of indebtedness—personal, mortgage, municipal, and provincial—were particularly difficult to bear with their high, fixed interest charges in a deflationary period. By 1935, the hopelessness of this situation had created an air of desperation to which politicians had to respond and which even the most selective editing of newspaper stories could not disguise effectively. The U.F.A. government could scarcely be blamed for the deteriorating economic climate, but they could not ameliorate it either, and for this they were held to account. Their greatest strength was their fervour for honest reform rooted in moral rectitude befitting an age in which social and economic change threatened to destroy a traditional way of life unless the guardians of tradition, in the face of indifference on the part of national governments, girded up their loins to do battle against the forces of modernization. In a depression, honesty and rectitude were not enough. Where Albertans had once contented themselves in demanding reform, they were now, as Macpherson concludes, "reduced to asking for relief..." [2]

As if to make matters worse for the U.F.A. government, just prior to the 1935 election it was publicly discredited by the personal behaviour of some of its leaders. The Premier, J.E. Brownlee, was sued in 1934 for seducing his young secretary, the daughter of a U.F.A. official of high standing in the Edson community. Simultaneously, the Provincial Treasurer's ex-wife appealed their divorce judgment, adding salacious speculation to overt scandal and providing considerable temptation to the more sensational elements among the press. Although these developments were usually reported in constrained and circumspect tones, their implications clearly offended the fundamentally conservative moral values of most Albertans. The two ministers resigned, but their cases dragged out over the election period with disastrous consequences for the government. Worse, both former ministers decided to participate personally in the campaign of 1935 thereby inviting the explicit moral condemnation of their constituents.

In the meantime, the same religious and moral values which the leaders of the U.F.A. had offended, and the economic dislocation which the U.F.A. had been unable to stem, were coming together in a wider conjuncture of individuals and circumstances which would help to create an environment – social, economic, political, and emotional – in which the Social Credit movement could prosper. The Canadian prairies were not only an area of reformist and populist politics, but they also shared with the North American west generally a fundamentalist, evangelistically-oriented, Protestant sectarianism. William Aberhart, the founder and leader of the Social Credit movement in Alberta, was an ardent evangelist, lay preacher, and Sunday School teacher who had the charismatic personality to ignite this latent fundamentalism. Nevertheless, his political appeal, which was inextricably intertwined with his religiosity, also extended to Catholics, Anglicans, Mormons, members of the United Church of Canada, and others – a strong argument against simple associations between political and religious fundamentalism.

Aberhart, born in Ontario in 1878, was a teacher by profession. Moving from Ontario to Alberta in 1910, he soon impressed Calgary's school officials with his administrative talents and in 1915 became the first principal of the newly created north-side Crescent Heights High School. Proud of his organizational talents (as he said, "It's a hobby with me"),[3] he ran the high school on weekdays and devoted his spare time to organizing Bible classes. At first working with local churches, in 1918 he organized his own Prophetic Bible Conference as an antidote to what he regarded as the too modernistic teachings of the established Protestant churches. Soon he was using the newly developed medium of radio to speak to an expanded audience over the clear air waves of southern Alberta on station CFCN, at the same time employing the mails to organize Bible study programs for his listeners. The Prophetic Bible Institute, of which Aberhart was president and dean, was completed in 1926, just three years before the depression began.

Until 1932, Aberhart continued his work in both secular and religious education, sheltered from the depression by his relatively secure principal's position. In that year, however, a number of events seemed to influence him profoundly. There was a controversy in Calgary over schoolteachers' salaries, followed by a general salary cut. Then, one of Aberhart's best students committed suicide "owing to his family's wretched circumstances".[4] Shortly after, while in Edmonton, a fellow summertime matriculation examiner introduced Aberhart to a popular version of the doctrines of Social Credit and expressed confidence that Aberhart was the right man to promote the message.

The theories of Social Credit were alien and distant from the sources Aberhart was accustomed to read, but they were a new Revelation. They were the creation of Major C.H. Douglas, a Scottish army engineer. His basic premise that money was merely the creation of governments or lending institutions, though unorthodox at the time, would not seem particularly controversial in our own day. But in a time of depression and deflation compounded by fiscal conservativism, an increased money supply was a revolutionary answer. The theories of John Maynard Keynes and the application of the "pump-priming" principle by government spending, as in the New Deal of Franklin Roosevelt in the United States, were analogous, up to a point. Douglas, however, emphasized priming the individual consumer through a system of "social dividends" derived from the state's manipulation of the credit represented by the natural, technological, or scientific resources which were part of society's "cultural heritage". The inflationary impact of providing individuals with the purchasing power associated with the equitable distribution of this "social credit" would be limited by the simultaneous imposition of controls such as the establishment of a "just price" on all commodities and stricter laws against usury. The enforcement of these controls, however, represents some of the murkier parts of Douglas' logic.[5]

Once William Aberhart had digested, to his own satisfaction, the theory of Social Credit, he used his skills as a teacher and as a preacher of simple formulae of salvation to present to the public an uncomplicated view of the meaning and working of Social Credit. He rarely referred specifically to Douglas' writings, emphasizing instead the promises of "social dividends" within the context of safeguards for the sanctity of private property and individual rights. More to the point, perhaps, Aberhart's Social Credit was explained, not in terms of technical detail, but through simple analogies, such as his comparison of the distribution of the money supply to the action of the heart pumping millions of gallons of blood – the same four quarts of blood – through the human body; or of Pat and Mike downing two kegs of whisky and paying for each drink, and hence for the two kegs, by passing the same quarter back and forth between them.

For the more sophisticated high-school graduate, there was Aberhart's version of Major Douglas' famous A plus B theorem, easily comprehended by anyone who remembered the clear logic of Euclidian geometry, a subject at which Aberhart must have excelled in his teaching career. If A plus B constituted the total cost of the factors of production and A was the factor of wages, salaries, and dividends, by simple logic, if not complex economics, the factors represented by A could never buy goods costing A plus B.

Another part of Aberhart's exposition of the Douglas theory was the focus of blame for economic conditions upon conspiratorial forces. Here was a tradition shared among the inheritors of the populist heritage, Social Credit doctrine and "fire and brimstone" fundamentalism, all of which Aberhart personified. The Devil, in this instance, was represented by the international forces of finance. Douglas soon focused upon the Jews in this context, as did some American Populists, but Aberhart did not share that particular prejudice. Aberhart, who had also read the speeches of William Jennings Bryan, chose to blame "the unscrupulous hosts of the Golden Moloch ...an octopus whose deathly blood sucking feelers are always extended to grasp us down to despair and misery."[6]

In the actuality of small-town and rural Alberta the clearly visible representatives of this evil force were the banks, whose national charters were carefully limited in number by the Canadian government. And, among the overt supporters of the banks were the newspapers. To combat these twin means of economic oppression, Aberhart preached the "intelligent" and "scientific" application of Social Credit doctrine, which included the possibility of limiting the freedom of the press and of controlling financial institutions. Ultimately, it was the means which Aberhart chose to control the banks and public opinion which caused the Social Credit experiment to fail in its economic objectives by 1938. This very failure, however, which could be attributed to a hostile press and the West's perennial bogeyman, the federal government, made Aberhart's political and moral objectives all the more real among a people long since convinced of a conspiracy against its right to pursue its own interests.

In the meantime, William Aberhart and his followers fought and won the election of 1935 in a campaign which, in the end, had less to do with Social Credit theory than with his plea for a personal mandate to reform the system, his popularity as a radio evangelist, and his carefully organized network of constituency workers who were frequently his devoted students as well. And in the long run it was the personal element in the relationship between the man and the people of Alberta, rather than Social Credit philosophy, which would determine how Aberhart interpreted his mandate. Direct democracy again emerged as the essential ingredient in Albertan politics and government.

II

As the Social Credit drama unfolded after 1935, it was reported and appraised daily in the Alberta press. There were four major daily newspapers in Alberta: the *Journal* and *Bulletin* in Edmonton, the *Herald* and the *Albertan* in Calgary. There were, as well, a host of rural and small-town papers – Lethbridge and Medicine Hat supported dailies and the rest were weeklies. The four leading newspapers had the broadest circulation, however, and the facilities for the most complete coverage of provincial news.

Learned treatises have been written on the impact of the press upon public opinion and behaviour. Students here may draw their own conclusion, contrasting in the first instance the editorial positions of most of the newspapers with the election returns. They should also take note, however, of those who have consistently criticized newspapers for their propensity to deal in stereotypes and clichés, appealing to the lowest common denominator among the reading public rather than performing a public educational function in the community.

Applying these standards to the urban press of Alberta in the nineteen-thirties, students should note the marked difference between news stories which describe events selected for inclusion by an editor, and editorials, in which editorial opinion is expressed freely. In the cases of the Edmonton *Journal* and the Calgary *Herald*, a certain similarity of viewpoint was to be expected as these newspapers were owned by the same syndicate, the Southam Press, a family-owned concern with headquarters in Montreal. In both cases hostility to the Social Credit movement and its leader were evident, though the *Journal,* under publisher John Imrie, was much more moderate in its criticism. Hostility sharpened during the 1937 period of challenge to the freedom of the press but rarely was it uttered in the vituperative tones expressed by the *Herald,* under publishers James Woods and O. Leigh-Spencer. A curious note on the decentralized editorial policy of the Southam newspapers can be added here. In Ottawa, the Southam's newspaper, the *Citizen,* edited by Charles Bowman, was an ardent supporter of Douglas' Social Credit theories throughout the twenties. In his memoirs, Bowman claims that two of the Southam brothers sponsored a speaking trip by Douglas to Canada in 1923. When Aberhart came to power Bowman remained sympathetic to Social Credit in Alberta, though he had misgivings about Aberhart's simplified adaptations of the Douglas theories. Yet, *Citizen* editorials expressing support for Aberhart were rarely reprinted in the Alberta Southam newspapers, which remained consistently, and often violently, opposed to Social Credit.

The other two newspapers held the less affluent morning market in their respective cities. The Edmonton *Bulletin*, founded in 1880, was the Liberal party's principal supporter over a span of many years. It upheld the Liberal platform in 1935, which paralleled Social Credit monetary theories to some extent in advocating use of federal money to fight the depression, but was nevertheless consistent in its support of Liberal politicians at both federal and provincial levels. In the years that followed its publisher, Charles Campbell, seemed to be grasping at issues to maintain reader support. These included limited working hours legislation, the Labour government of New Zealand as a model for Canada, and sympathetic coverage of the Spanish Loyalists and Chinese Communists as reported from the scene by Norman Bethune. And, in what may have been an unconscious contradiction of a left-wing editorial slant, the *Bulletin* ran more features from United States sources than the other newspapers, including cartoons and comic strips, the most rabidly right wing of which was "Little Orphan Annie".

Although somewhat more consistent editorially, the *Albertan* in this period was in a worse financial situation. Almost continuously from 1932 through 1935 its existence was subsidized by the *Herald* in order "to keep the fields stabilized", that is, to keep the morning *Albertan* out of direct competition with the afternoon *Herald*.[8] In early 1936 the Social Credit leaders made an arrangement whereby stock in the *Albertan* would be sold to supporters and the movement would thus have a daily paper of its own, publishing the *Alberta Social Credit Chronicle*, the propaganda medium, as a weekly supplement. The stock did not sell in adequate amounts and, when the press control legislation was proposed in 1937, the *Albertan* declared its independence of Social Credit. By 1939, the financial arrangement lapsed and the paper reverted to Max Bell, the son of the owner who had made the original arrangement.

These were the business aspects of the newspaper business in Edmonton and Calgary, but what of the contents of the papers themselves? Generally, the goal of editors and publishers was to maintain circulation and advertising revenue in a depressed economy by means of diverting readers from the dismal economic scene, the realities of which were too evident in their daily lives. The classified sections were atrophied but the big advertisers were still the automobile dealers annually promoting the new cars which few buyers could afford, and the department stores, which consistently bought entire pages throughout the year. These same large chain stores were among the targets of the 1934 Royal Commission on Price Spreads, whose report was inspired by charges of plenty in the midst of poverty levelled by Conservative Minister of Trade and Commerce, Harry Stevens. The report, which indicated that huge profit spreads existed between the prices paid for goods at wholesale and the retail prices in the stores, was not circulated with great enthusiasm by a daily press dependent on the stores' heavy advertising.

Front-page news sold the newspapers on the streets, not advertising. Rarely was an Alberta news story worth a banner headline, although the first years of Social Credit rated a few. The tendency of the press was to simplify issues and to sensationalize and dramatize events. Reading about other people's troubles helped divert readers from their own, and the remoteness of events from Alberta was a minor inhibition for an editor who wanted a sensational story. In fact, what passed for popular culture seems to have been imported from the United States. It was apparent in the most sensational story of 1935 and 1936 – the Lindbergh kidnapping. The infant son of the famous American flyer was kidnapped and murdered. The man responsible for these acts was tried, convicted, and went through numerous stays of execution in New Jersey. The glare of publicity in all aspects of this case still raises some doubts to this day regarding the quality of the justice exhibited there, but Alberta shared the vicarious thrills of the stories. The execution of Bruno Richard Hauptmann, like accounts of similar executions, or stories of executions, fits into a classic pattern of popular literature that has changed little over the centuries.

In a lighter vein, though the politicians of Canada were men whose privacy was generally respected, their speeches and public actions were accorded some space. Movie stars in contrast, however, received lavish coverage, and the Canadian press also gave celebrity treatment to royalty, particularly the British royal family. One continuing drama which unfolded involved first, King George V's twenty-fifth anniversary on the throne, followed by the sombre mourning of his death. The succession of King Edward VIII, the glamorous bachelor king who reigned for less than a year and then abdicated under most romantic circumstances, followed. Finally, the solid family of King George VI brought a happy conclusion to the royal pageant, including full-coverage of his coronation and the royal visit to Canada. Here was evidence of the fundamental British allegiance, particularly in Alberta, which was to develop much more tangible qualities with the outbreak of World War II in 1939. The newspapers also gave extensive coverage to the surrogate royalty of Canada, the Governors-General, whose travels were described in detail.

Alberta also had some colourful and newsworthy public figures of its own to compete for coverage, when their personal misfortunes were brought into court. In June 1934, the premier himself, Hon. John E. Brownlee, was the defendant in a civil suit charging seduction. The *Journal*'s John Imrie ordered his staff to write news articles "fit for a twelve-year-old girl to read",[9] but to make the charges clear to adults. The *Bulletin*'s reporter, J.S. Cowper, indulged in a more florid style, which cost him a contempt of court citation:

> She pictured the Premier of Alberta as a love-torn sex-crazed victim of passion and jealousy, forcing his will upon her in parked autos on country highways, making Sunday morning assignations ...flying into passions of rage when she attempted to deny him or to free herself from the tangled web of lust into which she had been drawn by his pleadings when a girl of eighteen.

> But a glance at the drawn face of Premier Brownlee as he sat by his counsel while the young witness told the story of the attentions he had showered on her—the meetings inside and outside the Parliament Buildings—the drives in the country—the days spent at his home when his family was away—even to his own admission that he had kissed her on occasions—showed how deeply charged the moment was for him. By his side sat his invalid wife, the most tragic figure of all in the crowded courtroom.[10]

Of much greater significance than any of this, of course, was the international news, which became increasingly more menacing as world crises unfolded from 1935 to 1939. The press in this period provided in generous supply and with considerable prescience the details of the events leading to World War II, even though newspaper readers may not have anticipated the end result. Commencing with Mussolini's invasion of Ethiopia in 1935 and parallel events involving Japan in China, through the Austrian annexation and the Czech crises, and culminating in 1938 with the general hope of people and press that Neville Chamberlain had achieved peace, the newspaper accounts still constitute the standard interpretation of the causes of that war.

These broader events also increasingly restricted press attention to the provincial politics of Alberta, especially after the courts and the federal government had curbed the extensive claims of power of the Social Credit forces. When the war that was a threat in 1938 became a reality in 1939, the media had less space for Canadian politics and even less yet for Alberta politics. Nevertheless, it also seems clear that, although

William Aberhart was to live until 1943, to be succeeded by his associate, Ernest Manning, who in turn became the longest tenured provincial premier in Canadian history, by 1938 other more recent public issues had begun to place Social Credit in Alberta in a much more limited, and a much less sensational, perspective.

III

The selections that follow are divided into three sections, each of which is arranged chronologically. The first, "The Road to Power, 1934-1935", provides what background can be rescued from the press reports of a man whose movement was promoted most effectively over the air waves. Major Douglas plays a personal role here, as the U.F.A. government had employed him in 1934 as an advisor to outflank Aberhart (Section I, document 4). The *Herald* still listed the Prophetic Bible Institute on its religious page, but soon dropped that practice and reported the political news from that location. In the north, Aberhart's reputation was so limited that the *Journal* ran a background feature (Section I, document 10). The balance of the section describes the political conflict and ultimate victory of Social Credit in the election of August 1935. The national implications of that success are evident in the final selections of the section. Opposition Leader Mackenzie King, facing strong opposition from both Social Credit and C.C.F. forces, was purposely conciliatory, campaigning in his own riding in Saskatchewan. Prime Minister R.B. Bennett, an old acquaintance of Aberhart, was uncompromising.

Section II, "Schism and the Backbenchers' Revolt, 1935-1937", focuses on the eighteen-month lull following the election of 1935, and leading to an open break in the Social Credit Party. In early 1937 the Edmonton *Journal* offered a rare compliment to Aberhart for his fiscal orthodoxy but the same day the Calgary *Herald* noted the radical proposals of the uninvited English Social Credit "expert" John Hargrave. (Section II, documents 8,9.) Hargrave was a key influence upon the backbench members of the legislature who were determined to press Aberhart for the implementation of Social Credit measures. Hargrave's personal frustration was indicated in his hasty departure on January 25, 1937. When the legislature met in March the reporters did their best to cover the rapidly occurring developments, a summary of which may be traced in Harold Schultz' article, collating the various press reports. As Schultz notes, Aberhart's "most effective weapon" was the air waves. One printed exposition of his position is contained in the Edmonton

Journal (Section II, document 16). The backbench insurgents wanted their social dividends and Aberhart yielded to them, reconstituting a board of "experts" from among their ranks to prepare bills for the session to follow. Aberhart, the schoolmaster who now had a rebellion in his class, was developing the skills of a politician, which included the willingness to compromise and yield when the alternative was the loss of power.

Section III, "The Press, The Courts, and The Constitution, 1936-1938", deals with the confrontations between the Alberta provincial government and the federal government, over the issues of bank regulation, press control, and delegating power to Social Credit boards. The sequence of events involved two further sessions of the legislature in 1938: the first in June 1937 to pass bank control legislation, which was disallowed by the federal government on the basis of its power under Section 90 of the British North America Act; and the second in August to pass a reworded bank regulation act (the Credit of Alberta Regulation Act), a press control act, and a new measure to licence businesses. In this last session of 1937, the Lieutenant Governor, J.C. Bowen, on advice from the federal Minister of Justice, Ernest Lapointe, took the highly unusual step of refusing to sign the bills, reserving them for quick reference to the Supreme Court of Canada and ultimate disallowance by the federal government.

The constitutional issue pressed by the Alberta government was that the powers of reservation and disallowance had lapsed with the course of time. The real political issues were illustrated by Lapointe's inconsistent application of the power of disallowance in Alberta's cases by refusing to support disallowance of the province of Quebec's 1937 *Act Respecting Communistic Propaganda,* commonly known as the Padlock Law, which clearly gave authoritarian power to the Attorney-General of Quebec to declare who were and who were not Communists. The C.C.F. spokesman, David Lewis, makes this point devastatingly well in Section III, document 21. The press was understandably most concerned about legislation that affected them directly, and thundered broadsides at the Aberhart government while proclaiming the virtues of a free press. The Pulitzer Prize committee's awards were a climax to their efforts (Section III, document 44).

The documents collected here raise a number of questions that to this day are difficult to resolve. The first concerns Aberhart's sincerity in promoting constitutional challenges that were clearly pressed upon him by his followers. His sincerity was not in question at any other time, but there are moments when a leader must become a follower. Further, did the Alberta government leaders expect the federal government to acquiesce to their demands, particularly when such powerful interests as the chartered banks and the press were challenged? Or, did they anticipate these developments and hope that the rebuffs would provide them with political ammunition for a national political campaign? Why did Aberhart challenge the appointment of the Rowell-Sirois Commission (Section III, document 23), a group selected to investigate discrepancies between federal taxing power and limitations upon the social use of tax money? His government refused to cooperate with its proceedings, publishing its own *Case for Alberta,* and when a Dominion-Provincial conference was called in 1940 to deal with the final report, Aberhart took advantage of the forum to assert his own solutions to the problems of the taxing powers of the state. Yet the Rowell-Sirois Commission was grappling with precisely the issues which Aberhart had capitalized upon in his ascent to power. These and other questions are raised by the documents. There remain a large variety of answers.

Notes to Introduction

1. C.B. Macpherson, *Democracy in Alberta, the Theory and Practice of a Quasi-Party System* ("Social Credit in Alberta, Its Background and Development", no. 4 [Toronto: University of Toronto Press, 1953]), pp. 3-27.

2. *Ibid.,* p. 7.

3. Harold Schultz, "Aberhart the Organization Man," *Alberta Historical Review,* VII (Spring, 1959), 20.

4. John Irving, *The Social Credit Movement in Alberta* ("Social Credit in Alberta. ..." no. 10 [Toronto: University of Toronto Press, 1959]), pp. 46-47.

5. See John Finlay, *Social Credit, Its English Origins* (Montreal: McGill-Queen's University Press, 1972), pp. 88-116.

6. *Alberta Social Credit Chronicle,* August 3, 1934.

7. Charles Bowman, *Ottawa Editor* (Sidney: Gray's Publishing Ltd., 1966), p. 187.

8. Charles Bruce, *News and the Southams* (Toronto: Macmillan, 1968), p. 296.

9. *Ibid.,* p. 288.

10. Edmonton *Bulletin,* June 24-25, 1934.

11. Harold Schultz, "The Social Credit Back-benchers' Revolt, 1937," *Canadian Historical Review,* XLI (March, 1960), 1-18.

12. John Saywell, "Reservation Revisited: Alberta 1937," *Canadian Journal of Economics and Political Science,* XXVII (August, 1961), 372.

Guide to Documents

SECTION I The Road to Power, 1934-1935

1. Camrose People Greet Social Credit Leader. *Alberta Social Credit Chronicle,* August 10, 1934.

2. The Discipline of Privation and Starvation (by William Aberhart). *Calgary Albertan,* November 2, 1934.

3. The Blood Stream of the State. *Calgary Albertan,* November 16, 1934.

4. An Indefensible Political Move. *Edmonton Journal,* February 25, 1935.

5. Chaos in Social Credit. *Edmonton Bulletin,* April 4, 1935.

6. Aberhart Should Accept Invitation. *Calgary Herald,* April 3, 1935.

7. Aberhart Social Creditors Draft Election Planks. *Calgary Herald,* April 6, 1935.

8. Aberhart Claims Overwhelming Support. *Edmonton Journal,* April 6, 1935.

9. The Social Credit Convention. *Winnipeg Free Press,* April 6-7, 1935, edited and reprinted in *Calgary Herald,* April 9, 1935.

10. Strong Personality (by Homer H. Ramage). *Edmonton Journal.* April 8, 1935.

11. Where is Money to Come From? *Calgary Herald,* April 9, 1935.

12. Deliberate Deception by U.F.A. *Edmonton Bulletin,* April 23, 1935.

13. Aberhart Speaks in Calgary. *Calgary Albertan,* April 23, 1935.

14. Aberhart Invokes Boycott. *Calgary Herald,* April 29, 1935.

15. Cults, Isms of West Irk Hanson. *Edmonton Bulletin,* May 1, 1935.

16. Alberta Faces Strange Election. *Calgary Herald,* July 17, 1935.

17. Social Credit Candidates Named. *Calgary Herald,* July 23, 1935.

18. Foretaste of What Will Happen. *Edmonton Journal,* July 24, 1935.

19. Social Creditors Lacking in Humour. *Calgary Herald,* July 26, 1935.

20. Calgary Board of Trade and Social Credit. *Calgary Herald,* August 8, 1935.

21. Chamber's Impressive Warning. *Edmonton Journal,* August 8, 1935.

22. The One Way Out—A Liberal View. *Edmonton Bulletin,* August 14, 1935.

23. If Aberhart Should Win. *Edmonton Journal,* August 15, 1935.

24. Reasons to Vote for Social Credit. *Alberta Social Credit Chronicle,* August 16, 1935.

25. Aberhart and the Election. *Edmonton Journal,* August 16, 1935.

26. Social Credit Wins Election. *Calgary Herald,* August 23, 1935.

27. Aberhart Denies Confiscation Charge. *Edmonton Bulletin,* August 24, 1935.

28. Aberhart Pleads for Support. *Calgary Herald,* September 16, 1935.

29. Poor Publicity for Alberta. *Calgary Herald,* September 17, 1935.

30. Bennett's Views on Aberhart. *Edmonton Bulletin,* October 4, 1935.

SECTION II Schism and the Backbenchers' Revolt, 1935-1937

1. Premier Promises Dividends. *Edmonton Bulletin*, December 23, 1935.
2. Aberhart and the Budget. *Albertan Social Credit Supplement*, February 22, 1936.
3. Douglas Resigns. *Edmonton Journal*, March 2, 1936.
4. All Strictly Orthodox. *Edmonton Bulletin*, March 3, 1936.
5. New S.C. Jargon Being Developed. *Calgary Herald*, March 10, 1936.
6. Hope in Alberta's Effort. *Ottawa Citizen*, April 10, 1936.
7. A Technical Default. *Calgary Herald*, April 21, 1936.
8. Premier's Reassuring Denial. *Edmonton Journal*, January 2, 1937.
9. Social Credit Could Work Successfully. *Calgary Herald*, January 2, 1937.
10. S.C. League to Discuss Resolutions. *Calgary Herald*, January 15, 1937.
11. Social Credit? *Calgary Herald*, January 15, 1937.
12. Frankness from Premier. *Calgary Herald*, January 15, 1937.
13. Aberhart Says Interest Cut: Fight to Proceed. *Albertan*, January 25, 1937.
14. Hargrave Leaves Edmonton: Aberhart's Response. *Calgary Herald*, January 26, 1937.
15. Why Not a General Election? *Calgary Herald*, March 2, 1937.
16. No Dividends and None in Prospect. *Edmonton Journal*, March 2, 1937.
17. S.C. Member Criticizes Government. *Calgary Herald*, March 5, 1937.
18. Time to Be Cautious. *Albertan*, March 6, 1937.
19. Fireworks Ahead. *Calgary Herald*, March 17, 1937.
20. Board to Have Wide Powers of Control. *Edmonton Journal*, March 17, 1937.
21. Aberhart Defends His Policies. *Edmonton Bulletin*, March 22, 1937.
22. Aberhart Should Resign. *Calgary Herald*, March 23, 1937.
23. Conflict Occurs Over Budget. *Calgary Herald*, March 23, 1937.
24. The Art of the Possible. *Edmonton Journal*, March 24, 1937.
25. The Awakening. *Calgary Herald*, March 24, 1937.
26. Government to Resign? *Calgary Herald*, March 25, 1937.
27. Cabinet May Seek $3,000,000. *Calgary Herald*, March 27, 1937.
28. S.C. Insurgents to Defeat Government? *Edmonton Journal*, March 29, 1937.
29. They Both Win. *Calgary Herald*, March 31, 1937.
30. Further Conflict Within the Ranks. *Edmonton Journal*, April 1, 1937.
31. Restraining Influences. *Calgary Herald*, April 5, 1937.
32. The Social Credit Board. *Calgary Herald*, April 12, 1937.
33. Premier Wields Big Stick Again. *Edmonton Journal*, April 20, 1937.

SECTION III The Press, the Courts, and the Constitution, 1936-1938

1. Statements on Social Credit Criticized. *Albertan*, January 6, 1936.
2. Penalty of Fame. *Edmonton Journal*, January 14, 1936.

3. Social Credit Party's Daily Organ. *Edmonton Journal,* January 16, 1936.

4. Aberhart Scores Press Regulations. *Edmonton Journal,* February 5, 1936.

5. Mr. Aberhart and the Press. *Albertan,* September 15, 1936.

6. Dictators and the Press. *Calgary Herald,* May 4, 1937.

7. Implementation of S.C. Program. *Edmonton Journal,* August 3, 1937.

8. One Astounding Bill Before House. *Edmonton Journal,* August 4, 1937.

9. True Democracy Dawns in Alberta? *Today and Tomorrow,* August 5, 1937.

10. Bank Control Bill. *Edmonton Journal,* August 5, 1937.

11. Shaking the World. *Calgary Herald,* August 6, 1937.

12. Back to the Middle Ages! *Edmonton Journal,* August 6, 1937.

13. Ousting of Mr. Hugill. *Edmonton Journal,* August 7, 1937.

14. Social Credit and Banking. *Edmonton Bulletin,* August 9, 1937.

15. Running Wild. *Calgary Herald,* August 12, 1937.

16. Dominion Cabinet Ruling. *Calgary Herald,* August 12, 1937.

17. Premier Dumfounded. *Edmonton Journal,* August 16, 1937.

18. Act is Invasion of Federal Field. *Edmonton Bulletin,* August 18, 1937.

19. Socred to Fight Ottawa Edict. *Edmonton Bulletin,* August 18, 1937.

20. Aberhart Challenges Federal Right of Disallowance. *Calgary Herald,* August 20, 1937.

21. Disallowance Draws Fire from C.C.F. *Edmonton Bulletin,* August 23, 1937.

22. Mandate of the People. *Edmonton Journal,* August 23, 1937.

23. New Protest by Aberhart. *Edmonton Bulletin,* August 27, 1937.

24. More Legislation Planned. *Edmonton Bulletin,* August 30, 1937.

25. M.L.A.s Study New Bills at Edmonton. *Albertan,* September 27, 1937.

26. An Extraordinary Bill. *Calgary Herald,* September 28, 1937.

27. Government Control of the Press? *Edmonton Bulletin,* October 1, 1937.

28. The Gag. *Calgary Herald,* October 1, 1937.

29. The Press Bill. *Albertan,* October 4, 1937.

30. Assent Withheld. *Edmonton Journal,* October 5, 1937.

31. Don't Raise that Issue. *Edmonton Bulletin,* October 6, 1937.

32. King Withholds Comment. *Albertan,* October 6, 1937.

33. Aberhart to Call an Election? *Edmonton Bulletin,* October 7, 1937.

34. Press Gag Opposed. *Calgary Herald,* October 12, 1937.

35. Aberhart Asks for Court Ruling. *Edmonton Journal,* October 18, 1937.

36. Credit Must be Controlled. *Edmonton Bulletin,* October 25, 1937.

37. Federal Cabinet Favours Court Ruling. *Edmonton Journal,* November 2, 1937.

38. Legal Array Set for Hearing. *Edmonton Journal,* January 5, 1938.

39. Judges Reserve Decision. *Edmonton Bulletin,* January 11, 1938.

40. Disallowance Acts Discussed. *Edmonton Bulletin,* February 5, 1938.

41. Supreme Court of Canada Ruling. *Edmonton Journal,* March 4, 1938.

42. Court Decisions Disappoint Premier. *Edmonton Journal,* March 4, 1938.

43. The Court's Decision. *Albertan,* March 5, 1938.

44. Alberta Papers Given Pulitzer Prizes. *Edmonton Journal,* May 2, 1938.

A Note on the Documents

Unless otherwise noted, the documents reproduced below conform in spelling, grammatical usage, and punctuation to the originals. Since *Canadian History Through the Press* is, in a limited sense, a history of Canadian journalism, it has seemed advisable to preserve contemporary usage, however questionable it might appear to be, in order to illustrate the changing quality of Canadian journalistic writing.

SECTION I

The Road to Power, 1934-1935

1 / CAMROSE PEOPLE GREET SOCIAL CREDIT LEADER

Alberta Social Credit Chronicle
August 10, 1934

More than 1500 people streamed in from a radius of thirty miles to Camrose arena and heard William Aberhart of Calgary expound his Social Credit remedy for the economic morass in which the province is sinking. For two hours this large gathering listened with close attention to the one man whose courageous leadership is lifting the heavy hand of despair from the people of the province.

With an oratory unexcelled in Canada, Aberhart asked the citizens of the district to put aside politics and partisanship and co-operate for at least one year. This, he claimed, was the only way to save the country from revolution or economic slavery.

Social Credit is not the socialization of financial credit, said Mr. Aberhart. This so-called panacea was simply putting a different man with a different colored pen in control of financial credit. To the man without real credit, it didn't really make the slightest difference.

Mr. Aberhart went on to say that the social credit of the people of Alberta was being exploited by the financial powers of today. The introduction of the system would only abolish the abuse of this tremendous power and return it to the hands of the people by whom it is created in basic dividends.

Answering the often asked question: where does all the money come from? Mr. Aberhart, with the able assistance of Mr. Manning, illustrated how he could buy a suit of clothes and pay his grocery bill without the payment of a single dollar. It is merely a cross entry in books, and if it works so neatly under the present system it should work the same way under the new order. The beauty of it all, thundered the speaker, is that it does not interfere with the Bank Act or that old bogy, the constitution.

Quoting a member of the Retail Merchants Association, Mr. Aberhart claimed that the cost of staples would be reduced 15 per cent under Social Credit. This would follow the removal of bad debts, the costs of collection, and a bigger turn-over. Farm machinery would be reduced from 30 per cent to 35 per cent for the same reasons.

This meeting was the second of his fourth week of touring the province. As he explains, it was not a political meeting. The purpose was purely educational. With two meetings a day Mr. Aberhart has spent the entire month of July on the road. He had no axe to grind, nor is he seeking personal favor and when one considers he is spending his holidays in this strenuous manner, it leaves no doubt as to his sincerity. The foregoing is typical of all similar meetings and in this connection we respectfully ask why we will not leave with [*sic*] social credit in the next election? There are many reasons for doing so and none against.

Mr. Aberhart has the absolute confidence of Social Credit of Alberta. As one dear old lady said: "I don't claim to understand the fine points of the system, but if Mr. Aberhart says it is so, I am sure everything will be all right."

It is a pleasure to feel the temper of the audiences. There were many, many thousands who will back him to the last ditch.

He is the originator of a plan which, based on Douglas principles, is the only one of its kind in North America. It is worthy of mention that it will not cost us $1200. When our self-styled leaders have been philandering, this man has been spending days of concentrated study on problems which are rightly theirs.

His heart burns for the welfare of the common man. It would be refreshing to have a churchman at the head of our government. Who is better fitted to carry out the teachings of Jesus Christ than a believer and doer of Christianity? This may be a novel idea for many of us but is worthy of consideration.

For the above and for many more reasons than is [*sic*] listed here, may we in Camrose venture to suggest that we voice the desire of thousands when we say, We Want Aberhart!

2 THE DISCIPLINE OF PRIVATION AND STARVATION

By William Aberhart, B.A.

Calgary Morning Albertan
November 2, 1934

In pagan countries, the great cure for sickness and ill-health was the infliction of torture or suffering to drive out the evil spirits. When medical science first began to invade the confines of this heathendom, the witch doctors opposed its introduction and warned against the evil results that must inevitably follow. For a time the poor natives were in abject fear, but gradually as one by one ventured to believe that no harm might come by trying these less painful remedies, and as cures began to manifest themselves in their midst, the witch doctors, who insisted on the compulsory pain and suffering of the unfortunate natives, were completely discredited and their thraldom was destroyed.

MODERN APOSTLES OF SUFFERING

In Alberta at the present time, in the face of the greatest enlightenment and scientific advancement of the age, there are still witch doctors, the modern apostles of suffering, who maintain that if we remove starvation and awful privation, the human race will be degraded by the influx of evil tendencies, the morale of mankind would be destroyed and people would become infernally lazy. They believe that to save the human race, and especially the unfortunate ones, we must keep them in a half-starved, half-clothed, unsanitary condition of living. If we were to give all the citizens monthly dividends sufficient to purchase the bare necessities of food, clothing and shelter, we would destroy their morale, and make them lazy.

Like the Israelites of old, we must force them to make bricks without straw to keep them underneath the authority of the powers that be. In this case it is the financiers instead of, as it was formerly, the Pharaohs of old Egypt.

FALSITY ON THE FACE OF IT

There are citizens today who receive dividends without working for them. Has their morale been broken? Have they no longer any ambition to exert their individuality? I have never seen a man yet who made $500 thus, who did not go after another.

If these fortunate individuals who have regular dividends coming to them are being so badly injured spiritually and morally, why not pass an act of parliament to prevent all dividends? We pass laws to prevent suicide and self-destruction. This would be in line if the claim is true. It is inconsistent to talk against dividends for all while we retain the dividends for the few. Since the citizens are associated in a co-operative state, which produces an unearned increment, why should any others receive the result of this cultural heritage? Why should any individual in our midst want to amass so much wealth that he or his heirs can never use it? Would it not be more reasonable and more pleasant to live and let the other fellow live also? Social Credit monthly dividends will remove poverty and privation. Then why should we not all desire it? Remember it deprives no one of his individual enterprise to earn enough to obtain all the luxuries he can enjoy.

The poorer folks will be glad to see you enjoying the best, and will be glad to serve you as long as they are not left in abject poverty and suffering.

BENEATH STATUS OF DUMB ANIMALS

We have a law on the statute books of the province of Alberta forbidding the starving or otherwise neglecting to care for dumb animals. Fines and imprisonment may be administered to anyone guilty of such awful cruelty to animals.

Since we allow human beings to starve and suffer from privation, are we to conclude that our governments consider human beings are beneath the status of the dumb animals?

Where will you find a psychologist today who would advise parents to starve and half-clothe their children in order to keep them obedient and good? That is the very opposite to the truth.

No parent body would be so cruel and viciously insane as to refuse sufficient food, clothing and shelter to his own offspring. If we found one, the authorities should arrest him and examine his sanity. Why then should any statesman (or should I say any party politician) openly tell the public that the citizens must be starved, ill-treated, and badly housed to keep them decent and respectable?

Such a suggestion is beneath the dignity and intelligence of present day civilization.

BUT IT WOULD PRODUCE LAZINESS

Once more we repeat that this charge is absolutely contrary to the truth. Treat people properly and they will respond.

If, however, an odd person would refuse to co-operate, after repeated warnings, his dividends might be suspended temporarily or permanently. If he still refused to work at all, he could be taken in as a vagrant and be made to work under rigid military discipline.

Our roads could be improved by these poor subnormal chaps who need the direction and discipline of the state officials. But they would be fed, clothed and sheltered.

What are we doing with such men today? They are receiving relief, it is true, but how many feel the urge to work. If they do, they at once lose part or all of their relief. It pays to be idle. Under Social Credit it would pay to work.

SOMETHING-FOR-NOTHING JOKE

But is this not giving them something for nothing? How superficial such a camplaint [sic] is! Who is getting the benefits of the unearned increment of association today? Have they more claim upon it than the bona fide citizens of our province?

I know many old timers who have slaved for twenty, thirty or even forty years in this province fighting pests, trying to evade hail and frost, and what have they to show for it? They have given the best part of their lives for the development of the province.

Now they have nothing but huge debts and may be turned out on the road in their old age. Is it giving them or their loved ones something for nothing if we guarantee them food, clothing and shelter?

There is no other proposal but Social Credit that attempts to cope with the present heart-breaking conditions. Once the people understand the workings of Social Credit, they recognize its matchless value.

If each Social Creditor becomes a booster

and all our citizens get a little insight into it, the next election will see it introduced.

---

3 THE BLOODSTREAM OF THE STATE

By William Aberhart, B.A.

Calgary Morning Albertan
November 16, 1934

The progress made in the realm of physical science during the last century has been phenomenal. So great has it become that many inventions, that are exquisitely wonderful and that will bring much enjoyment and leisure to mankind, have been deliberately shelved. The human race cannot afford to have them.

At the same time the progress in the economic and political sciences has woefully lagged behind. We are still using the same old system that was in vogue in the time of scarcity, before machinery had lifted the burden off the back of mankind. No wonder the physical scientists have been hampered in their endeavors to ameliorate the present unhappy conditions of the human race.

Someone has pictured the present situation as one comparable to a huge steam shovel dredging out an embankment to make a road while half a dozen men with wheel-barrows are vainly attempting to carry off the huge pile resulting from the steam shovel's operation. Is it any wonder that the wheels of production are compelled to be idle for a time. So it is with our present economic system. The machinery of production has become so modernized that the work supplying goods to feed, clothe and shelter our people has become comparatively easy. In fact so easy that we are vigorously struggling with other nations to obtain foreign markets to provide for their people as well. While at the same time, through inefficiency of our economic system we are unable to distribute the goods in our own land. To such an extent is this a disability that many of our people are undergoing privation and suffering from lack of the necessaries of life in the midst of the abundance piled high on the shelves of our warehouses and elevators.

Thus far our only suggestion is wantonly and insanely to destroy the goods or curtail further production.

23

Are we to admit that we have not brains enough to discover a scientific remedy for this outlandish condition?

SECRET OF SCIENTIFIC PROGRESS

A glance at the progress in the physical sciences will convince you that they have discovered a secret that we would do well to note carefully. Much of the progress has been due to the fashioning of our inventions in accord with the great models of Nature.

If we wish a camera, we fashion one after the structure of the human eye. If we are to have a telephone or a phonograph, we fashion them after the principles of the larnyx and the ear. If we are to fly above the earth, we do well to note carefully the flight of birds.

Why has the thought never dawned upon our economists to follow the same method of progress?

It was Major C.H. Douglas who, as a technical engineer, first suggested the comparison between the bloodstream of the body and the flow of credit in the state. It was he who coined the phrase in connection with the process of distribution that is often used to-day, viz., "the bloodstream of the state."

The flow of blood in the body well illustrates the function and the method of the flow of credit in the state. In the body, the blood flows out from the heart through the arteries to every part of the human system. Here it performs its function, i.e., to feed, clothe and shelter every cell of the body. At the same time it picks up any impurities of poisons and returns them to the heart, from whence it is once more forced out to the lungs for purification. After its purification it returns to the heart once more and begins all over again its proper functioning.

It is thus that the flow of credit must circulate. The heart of the province is the State credit house and not the banks or financiers. The credit will flow out from the credit house in two chief ways:

1. Credit loans will be given producers and distributors for the purpose of financing the production of the necessary goods. These loans will be without interest. No state can long survive the clutches of interest.

The credit thus given out by the State credit house will be paid out by the producers and distributors to the consumers in the form of wages, salaries, commissions, purchases of raw materials, general expenses, etc.

That is the producers and the distributors become the arteries of the state. The use of non-negotiable certificates issued by each citizen gives the State credit house the power of direction, that it could not have with the ordinary kinds of money.

2. This distribution by credit loans would not be sufficient to enable all citizens to purchase the necessities of food, clothing and shelter. If the modern machinery was used, there could never be found work for all.

Thus the State credit house would give to every bona fide citizen, basic monthly dividends to supplement the purchasing power of the consumers so that there would be sufficient to move all the goods. These dividends are the rightful claim of the cultural heritage in modern progress.

Thus the blood of the State, that is, credit buying power, would move through the purchase of goods, services, bonds, etc. A compulsory spending act could be introduced if necessary to prevent the accumulation of credit in the branch credit houses and thereby prevent one citizen or a group from inflating or deflating purchasing power at will.

This credit would rapidly flow from consumer to retailer and on to the wholesaler. From the wholesaler it would soon find its way to the producer who would return his loan to the State credit house from whence it came.

The basic dividends would be returned to the State credit house by the producer or wholesaler through an unearned increment levy. Much in the same manner that the gasoline or sales taxes are handled today.

WHERE WOULD CREDIT COME FROM?

The question that puzzles some who follow the system favorably thus far is this: Where will all the credit come from? Or would these credit loans not soon increase to such an amount that the province would be bankrupt?

Thus they figure. Twenty-five dollars a month for 400,000 citizens is a charge of ten million dollars. For a year would be 120 million. For 25 years would be three billion. According to the Canada Year Book 1933, the estimated wealth of Alberta is only $2,406,-000,000. Hence they say Alberta would be bankrupt in 25 years.

Suppose they reasoned thus with the blood stream of the body. The heart normally beats 72 times a minute, and pumps from four to six ounces each time (say five ounces).

The heart therefore pumps 360 ounces or nine quarts of blood per minute. This would be 540 quarts or 135 gallons per hour. If we continue our figuring for the day, the month, and the year, we find that the human heart pumps 1,182,600 gallons for the year, and in 25 years over 29 million gallons of blood. Where will any of us get this huge quantity of blood? Surely no man will be able to live for 25 years. This is absurd. Why?

The blood returns again and again to the heart. A person weighing 130 pounds has an average of about 10 pounds or four quarts of blood. Can we not all see how his heart will be able to pump 135 gallons of blood per hour with only four quarts of blood? The blood passes through the heart about twice a minute. It is the flow that does the trick.

SO IT IS WITH THE FLOW OF CREDIT

Money today, with all our depression, is flowing at the rate of one to 16 per year.

Raymond claims to have done $40,000 worth of business in one year with $400 of script, i.e., a rate of 1 to 100. I am satisfied that under Social Credit, the flow would probably exceed the present rate five times. But suppose it is only 1 to 12. All the credit that would be needed to handle our basic dividends would be about 10 million dollars. We are spending nearly that amount on interest payments of our mortgage indebtedness.

The unearned increment levy on our total production would but be from 2 to 3 per cent.

With a complete census of our provincial wealth, and population of today, this could be accurately discovered and applied.

Why not consider this matter in detail? The mental acumen of our inhabitants, I am sure, is great enough to figure out a satisfactory, scientific basis by which our goods and services could be distributed without the present loss and sabotage.

Be a booster for Social Credit!

4 AN INDEFENSIBLE POLITICAL MOVE

Edmonton Journal
February 25, 1935

There can be only one explanation of the decision of the provincial government to invite Major Douglas back to Alberta—that it has a purely political purpose in view. Mr. Aberhart and his followers propose to contest numerous constituencies at the coming general election. Because their social credit ideas have appealed strongly to a considerable proportion of those who have been in the habit of voting for candidates placed in the field by the U.F.A., that organization, it is evident, feels it to be necessary to try to retain their allegiance through arranging another visit from the old country economist.

The step that the government has taken was urged at last month's U.F.A. convention after the Aberhart proposals had been voted down by an overwhelming majority. Its object is so apparent that it is quite unlikely to have any large political effect. In any case to involve, for the sake of this, the province in the expenditure that will be entailed is altogether inexcusable. Nothing could have been made plainer than that the Douglas plan could not be worked out on a provincial basis. So why should the government or the legislature consider it further? They have surely enough to do in dealing with matters that are within their jurisdiction. Alberta's financial position is such as to demand all possible economies. How then can any justification be offered for spending a further sum in securing advice from Major Douglas after he was paid a fee of $1250 for that which he tendered last March?

A book of 127 pages has been printed and widely circulated by order of the legislature which contains the detailed evidence given before the agricultural committee at that time. A review of this appeared in "Prosperity," an English publication which, according to its own description, is issued "for the promulgation and establishment of the Douglas social credit proposals." Here is part of what the reviewer had to say:

On page 122 Douglas admits that social credit, "on account of your limited powers," could not be put into force in Alberta. This should prove conclusive evidence for any misguided enthusiasts who are pressing for a provincial application of some so-called social credit system in the province alone.

Then why bring Major Douglas back? With the stand that he took on the inability of the province to carry out his ideas all who followed the proceedings are familiar. In the light of this the only reasonable conclusion to be reached was that expressed by Mr. Duggan when he said:

Major Douglas made it perfectly clear that his social credit plan cannot be applied successfully in this province. His statements in that respect were disappointing to many but they served to remove the necessity for further consideration by the legislature.

In a radio address during the present month Mr. Priestley, the vice-president of the U.F.A., asked why Mr. Aberhart was attacking that organization almost exclusively.

Why does he not be fair, that official went on, and say that when the report of the agricultural committee was presented to the Alberta legislature covering the enquiry of last March and April into the various social credit proposals, including his Alberta scheme, not a single member of the sixty-three in the legislature voiced the belief that a feasible plan for Alberta had been set forth?

It was not to be expected that any of these sixty-three members, having agreed that no such plan had been presented and having been told so definitely by Major Douglas of the obstacles in the way of provincial action would now be in favor of having him make a return visit. The government, by arranging this, may help in diverting from the U.F.A. the attacks of the Aberhart group which Mr. Priestley was answering. But it must impair seriously as a consequence the support and confidence that it has hitherto won for itself in other quarters.

If it is the last word I speak in public, former Premier Brownlee told the United Farm Women of Alberta at Calgary last month in discussing social credit proposals, I would impress on you that nothing but disillusionment, loss of hope and additional despair can follow an attempt to inaugurate a system of that kind, because the province has no jurisdiction in these matters.

There was certainly no lack of frankness or vigor in this. About the same time the ex-premier urged Albertans not to be led away by "cheap politicians" and to face issues fairly and work through proper channels for monetary reform. But the present members of the government, in taking the step that was announced yesterday, have certainly left themselves sadly open to have applied to them the phrase which their former head used of those against whom he warned the people of the province.

5 CHAOS IN SOCIAL CREDIT

Edmonton Bulletin
April 4, 1935

Predicting "chaos and confusion" from any attempt to enforce the Aberhart plan of social credit in Alberta, ex-Premier J.E. Brownlee, in a radio address over station CJCA Wednesday night, declared that if such a plan were established the province "would probably be glad the British North America Act provides that the governor-general-in-council may disallow provincial legislation."

The former U.F.A. government leader invited contributions to pay for continuing the radio campaign, which, he declared, served "an excellent purpose in pointing out the many serious defects and deficiencies in the picture painted by the proponents of the Alberta system of social credit, notwithstanding the vividly rosy colors lavished on the canvas.

He concluded his broadcast with a questionnaire directed at Aberhardt [*sic*] followers.

He stated a series of broadcasts was planned to allow closer scrutiny of proposals by the people of the province before they endorse them.

In an examination of the "greatest economic cataclysm modern civilization has ever known," Mr. Brownlee said that despite falling prices to producers and all the other financial and economic evils that have followed, schools and hospitals have been maintained, government services have been continued and help has been provided for aged, for mothers and the needy.

"We have accomplished these things," he continued, "because we have maintained the integrity and credit of the province; we have worked in harmony with and not in defiance of the national government; we have not isolated this province from the general economy of the rest of Canada."

"Is it not our bounden duty to make sure we can protect these amenities before we rush blindly about seeking the pot of gold at the end of the rainbow."

He reviewed Mr. Aberhart's proposals for a $25 per month basic dividend; a just price for commodities, and a continuous flow of credit, as well as proposed loans to farmers of $1,500.

"Loans of $1,500 for 90,000 farmers amounts merely to $135,000,000, and $25 per month for 400,000 adults is only the trim little, tidy little sum of $120,000,000 per year. All that in a province of some 700,000 people still in the early development stage of its provincial life with few native corporations, few large incomes, and but comparatively small accumulation of wealth."

"Will someone page Mr. Upton Sinclair with his slogan 'Everyone Prosperous in California,' Dr. Townsend with his $200 per month at 60 years of age, and Mr. Huey Long with his motto 'Every Man a King?' They need the stimulus of the exhilarating, exuberant, intoxicating atmosphere of sunny Alberta.

"But that is the proposal and, Mr. Citizen, with your interest in the province, that is the issue. Can you remain indifferent to the threat it offers to the well-being of this province? Dare you risk the chaos and confusion that will result from any attempt to put it into effect?"

Dealing with the $25 basic dividend to take care of the "bare necessities," Mr. Brownlee declared the government had long since recognized its duty in seeing that its citizens were properly fed and clothed. The government accepted this responsibility and it was only through federal co-operation that the province had been able to shoulder the $2,264,747 cost of relief last year, he pointed out.

"But why pay dividends to provide such bare necessities to those who are amply provided?" he asked. "Why tax the people with one hand to hand back to some of them with the other that which they already have? Why pay basic dividends for example to those with incomes of $3,000 and upwards?"

He pointed out that Major Douglas now limits the application of the basic dividend to those receiving incomes under four times the basic dividend. The United Farm movement, however, had been favorable and sympathetic to the general principles of social credit, but only to the extent it affects monetary improvement so money might bring closer productive capacity and consumptive demand of produce.

"I frankly admit," he said, "that I am not in the habit of signing blank cheques. I will not therefore blindly subscribe to any plan simply because it carries with it the general trade name of social credit."

Claiming that he was supported by the Douglas Credit league of Canada and Major Douglas himself, Mr. Brownlee charged that any such plan could be enacted only by a sovereign state having complete control over its major financial institutions with full and complete powers of taxation and with equally full and complete control over trade and commerce.

He quoted from evidence taken in the legislature during Major Douglas' past visit here to substantiate his claim.

6 ABERHART SHOULD ACCEPT INVITATION

Calgary Herald
April 3, 1935

The public must be growing tired of the long range discussion between Premier Reid and William Aberhart concerning the legislature's invitation to the latter to go to Edmonton and submit his social credit plan to the consideration of the members.

It has become obvious to every unbiased observer that Mr. Aberhart is deliberately sidestepping the invitation and the opinion is becoming general that he has not the slightest intention of acceeding to the request of the legislature. He has been putting up objections, many of which are puerile and beside the mark. At first he said it would not be possible to place a comprehensive detailed plan of social credit before the people prior to the arrival of Major Douglas in May. He referred vaguely to assistance he expected from the government and to figures which might be made available.

Now hearing that the provincial election may be called in late May or early June, he informs Premier Reid: "This will not give me sufficient time to perform the task that you have invited me to do." The public generally, and Mr. Aberhart's followers particularly, may well ask for an explanation of this statement. What has Mr. Aberhart been doing in the past twelve months or more but proclaiming that he has a DEFINITE PLAN of social credit for Alberta? Why is he so vague and hesitant about essentials now? By a concentrated crusade through his pulpit every Sunday, and of late on Tuesday evenings, as well as at innumerable public gatherings, he has assured the people of this province that he has a definite plan to give every adult a basic dividend from the public credit. He has spoken authoritatively of just prices and basic dividends and unearned increment as if he knew all about them. He expressed complete and every confidence in his plan and he has raised hopes to a high pitch among his followers. He should not now be allowed to evade his responsibility. The present social credit expectations in this province were created solely by him, and he should welcome the opportunity to make good his promises before the legislature and the people at large.

Now he declares he cannot get away from pressing school duties to confer with the premier although the chairman of the school board, Mr. F. E. Spooner, says he will be granted leave of absence at any time in view of the importance of the mission. Mr. Aberhart, having fathered the social credit agitation, must see it through. He is the sole leader of the Aberhart campaign and he should run for the legislature and thus try to get into a position to complete his self-imposed mission. Nothing else would be fair to his supporters. With an election in sight he should go to Ed-

monton and explain to the House the plan he has been asking the people to support during the past two years. That is the only honorable course for him to pursue. He has already wasted one month since the legislature invited him in March 5, by raising technicalities that deceive no one.

---

7 ABERHART SOCIAL CREDITORS DRAFT ELECTION PLANKS

Calgary Herald
April 6, 1935

With some alterations, changes and deletions to the tentative draft prepared some time ago, Southern Alberta delegates to the social credit convention Friday adopted a 10-point platform.

On that platform disciples of the William Aberhart social credit theory will go to the people in the coming election. The same draft is expected to supply the background for the Northern Alberta convention decisions when delegates north of the Red Deer gather at Edmonton April 25-26.

In event of further changes being brought in by the northern convention, committees from both sections will meet in joint session at a date to be fixed to level off the varying planks.

Friday morning, last day of the convention at Calgary, delegates reviewed the draft platform, submitting numerous resolutions for amalgamation by the nominating committee, which in turn brought in proposals for 11 changes. Seven of these were approved, and shortly after 5 o'clock the election ammunition was all in order.

It was just shortly before that time, however, that a warning note crept into the meeting. It came while a clause calling for reduction in the number of members was under consideration and it served to show that the first social credit convention had founded the basis for the first rupture among followers.

A slim, elderly, gray-haired lady, Mrs. N. Campbell, who announced to the convention she was one of the seven sent in by Pincher Creek constituency, stood up and said she was taking her courage in her hands and was going to make an unpopular statement. It was, simply and quietly stated:

"The autocratic stand taken in the selection of candidates yesterday has caused a rift in social credit ranks." There was no comment except for a brief period of unusual silence.

Spectators' galleries and the centre section of the Bible Institute were comfortably filled, not crowded, as the convention settled down to the serious business of the agenda.

Before embarking on the resolutions pertaining to the several planks of the draft platform delegates were warned by Chairman Ernest C. Manning to keep to matters of policy and hold discussion to such points. He urged the convention not to ramble into matters of detail regarding administration of such policies.

Early in the discussion delegates voted down an amendment regarding finance and distribution of goods which asked substitution of the following for one of the original clauses. It suggested:

"The distribution of purchasing power to bona fide citizens in accordance with the basic principle of the Douglas system by means of basic dividends sufficient to cover the bare necessities of food, clothing and shelter."

Sponsors of the amendment held it would eliminate certain misunderstandings and refute arguments that the Aberhart system is not the same as the Douglas plan. Opponents said it would provide contentious matter for political argument, while considerable educational work remains to be completed.

Providing for everything from basic dividends to institution of recall legislation for erring members who gain a seat, the social credit platform calls for establishment of a "just price" on goods and services, that producers shall not be asked to sell goods for less than cost, and consumers not be exploited.

It promises, when opportunity is available, to extend the scope and operation of the Debt Adjustment Act to meet requirements of all classes of debtors and production loans passed upon by a board to be established.

Agricultural development by various means, reorganization of all government departments, more equitable freight rates and other sub-items four dozen in number comprise the platform.

8 ABERHART CLAIMS OVERWHELMING SUPPORT

Edmonton Journal
April 6, 1935

Eighty per cent of the electors of Alberta are behind Social Credit, and the forthcoming provincial general election will witness a landslide for this party, declared William Aberhart—who will be Alberta's next premier if this prediction comes true—at the final session Friday of the southern Alberta convention that launched Social Credit as a political party.

Mr. Aberhart devoted most of his time to hitting back at two of his chief critics, the Calgary Herald and J.E. Brownlee, former premier. Fourteen hundred persons jammed the Calgary Prophetic Bible Institute to hear Mr. Aberhart. And two overflow meetings, with radio connection, attracted other large crowds.

Any who expected Mr. Aberhart to elaborate on the Social Credit platform adopted earlier in the day was disappointed. Mr. Aberhart contented himself with speaking in general terms, reiterating that no definite plan had been drawn up yet; that no one need expect one plan to be perfect at first, and that the best men possible would be needed to get Social Credit working.

To the accompaniment of wild cheering, Mr. Aberhart vented his feelings on the criticism to which he has been subjected by the Calgary Herald and Mr. Brownlee.

He waved a recent editorial from the Herald. "Here they say: 'The mixing of religion and politics is never agreeable to the thoughtful observer and it cannot be doubted that the leader of this movement has used and is using a tabernacle built in the name of religion to promote what is rapidly becoming a political party.'

"That's a polite way of saying 'you know we are very religious down here at the Herald.'"

The crowd hooted and cheered.

"I have always believed that a religion worth anything should be practiced in every sphere of life," he asserted.

"The day is past for a religion that is worn like a cloak on Sundays and put on the shelf for the other days of the week. It may be that

I have offended the Herald by using this tabernacle to help the people of this province—but it ill becomes them to criticize our methods," he declared.

"The man who wrote that editorial hasn't the first idea of what Social Credit is. Whoever said we would have a perfect system to start with? We will have to watch every move carefully," he continued.

Mr. Aberhart remarked that Mr. Brownlee has developed into a violent anti-Social Creditite. The crowd booed at the mention of Mr. Brownlee and Mr. Aberhart scolded it for doing so.

"Booing," he said, "is a sign of lack of intelligence."

He said that every man had the right to express his opinion. If a person didn't want to hear it, he should rise and walk out."

Mr. Brownlee had said that chaos and confusion would result from an attempt to inaugurate the Aberhart plan of Social Credit in the province.

"Can Mr. Brownlee prevent chaos and confusion by any means at his disposal?" demanded Mr. Aberhart. "Let him tell how he will prevent chaos and confusion."

He remarked that Mr. Brownlee had argued that a new province of only 700,000 persons and a few native industries could not stand taxation of $120,000,000 a year to provide the basic dividend. The ex-premier had argued that blue ruin would attend Social Credit.

"Think of that as a statement from a man who took over the government when the provincial debt was $63,000,000 and then saw it grow to $144,000,000 while the revenue of the province was between $8,000,000 and $10,-000,000 a year. How can he say we will have blue ruin when he has given us blue ruin through interest-bearing debt?" demanded Mr. Aberhart.

Mr. Aberhart said that what he was interested in was Social Credit. It was not primarily essential that he should be the leader of the movement. Another could lead if he stood fast to the fundamental principles.

Every intelligent man in Canada, he said, knew about the "terrific" price spreads and "the interest charges beyond the ability of the people to pay." McGreer [sic] Stevens and others had exposed the "grafters."

"Cast your ballots right this time or you may never have a chance to cast them again," he warned. "Are you going to put the old line parties into power, or men and women who have the backbone to stand for deliverance of the people from economic slavery?"

Mr. Aberhart said he knew that even some delegates were going around saying: "We wish Aberhart would leave his religion out of this."

"I will not force my religion on anyone. No religion is worth a hill of beans if it is forced," he said.

Dealing with the question of what would be behind the first issue of Social Credit dividends, Mr. Aberhart asked: "What is behind the bonds you sell in New York now? The natural resources, of course. That is what will be behind our basic dividends."

9 THE SOCIAL CREDIT CONVENTION

ed. by J.B. McGeachy

Winnipeg Free Press
April 6-7, 1935
reprinted in Calgary Herald
April 9, 1935

Outside views are often of interest. The Winnipeg Free Press sent a staff representative to the Social Credit convention in this city last week, and the following is taken from his reports:

It is a common opinion in Calgary that William Aberhart, veteran high school teacher of this city, will form a new Alberta government after the provincial elections this summer. Mr. Aberhart heads the Alberta Social Credit League, now holding its first convention here. To his followers he is a divinely inspired leader to a promised land in which every adult will draw $25 a month without working for it. Others call him a Canadian Huey Long.

He was familiar to Alberta radio audiences as a prophetic orator before he took up Social Credit two years ago. Among the past prophecies credited to him are an Anglo-American alliance against the yellow races (1921), four-dollar wheat (1932), and the end of the world (1934).

Mr. Aberhart traces his economic gospel to

Major Douglas, originator of the Social Credit theory, but many Douglasites here repudiate him. They say Alberta, not controlling banking and currency, cannot try out the Douglas plan. They accuse Mr. Aberhart of failure to explain how he will raise the $120,-000,000 a year needed to pay the projected $25 monthly to everyone. Nothing said Thursday cleared up the mystery. No speaker came within a mile of the working of social credit. The Delegates, huddled on the floor of the church, are mainly from rural Alberta. All are imbued with the fervor of distressed people who have seen a vision.

On Thursday afternoon, Mrs. Frank Gostic, calling herself an "obedient soldier," taking orders from "the general" (meaning William Aberhart B.A.), wise-cracked for half an hour and wound up with a poem by Edgar Guest entitled "It Can Be Done." C.M. Wilmott, also on the light-hearted side, said that true love would flourish and there would be an end to the "hideous monstrosity of divorce." Under social credit, with a $25 monthly income of her own, Mr. Wilmott indicated, a woman would not have to marry for comfort, but could have the man of her choice. This was Mr. Wilmott in serious vein. Six resolutions passed later in the evening sketched the political plans of the Social Credit league and showed again Mr. Aberhart's absolute control. The league is going into the provincial elections and proceeds blithely on the assumption it will elect a majority.

In each constituency the league supporters are to nominate "three or four" men and then Mr. Aberhart, assisted by a central committee which seems unlikely to say much except "yes", is to choose the one he likes. This was the only debated proposal. A few bolder delegates thought it was undemocratic and suggested fascism, but a word from Mount Sinai settled the issue. Mr. Aberhart waited till his views were asked from the floor, then, rising with much gravity, he said: "If you're not going to allow me any say in the choice of my supporters, you're not going to have me as your leader."

The debate collapsed amid rapturous cheering for the inspired one.

Mr. Aberhart had sat in almost unbroken silence for two days, waiting like a prima donna to support the climax. He speaks fluently ...and with violent gestures, waving his arms and raising an admonitory finger when the applause has gone too far. Now and again he draws a large handkerchief from his sober black coat and mops a dome-like brow gleaming from his exertions.

He had his audience under perfect control, drawing laughter and cheers as from a tap. As a rabble-rouser he is in the top flight. When he hurled anathema at a Calgary newspaper which had criticized him, a scrubby old gentleman in the front pew of the church twitched his eyebrows, glared at the press table and shouted "Give 'em some more of that" the newspaper writers were glad to be separated from this bellicose customer by a thick hedge of brass tubas.

Remarkable were the omissions from Mr. Aberhart's speech. He did not trouble to acknowledge his "election" to the leadership of a political party.

He took it for granted also that the people in the pews and galleries knew what social credit meant and needed no instruction on its workings. His popularity rests on his confident statement that every adult, under social credit, can draw a "dividend" sufficient for the necessities of life. There was not a word in his speech to explain how this dividend (popularly expected to be $25 a month though Mr. Aberhart cautiously avoids the figure) is to be paid.

Another curious point about the speech was that the name of Major C.H. Douglas did not once creep into it. In fact Douglas was rarely mentioned by anyone at the convention, though he is supposedly the originator of the economics espoused by Mr. Aberhart. The explanation in Calgary is that Mr. Aberhart is not preaching Douglas economics but Aberhart economics, and that Major Douglas, when he comes to Alberta next month at the invitation of the Reid government, will spike the Aberhart guns by advising that his theory can only be tested properly on a national scale.

However that may be, Mr. Aberhart's rousing speech contained little light on what practical steps he would take if elected premier of the province. He predicted a landslide for his party in the elections. He denounced his critics. He defended himself for mixing religion and politics, and from the audience got a pointer for future speeches when a woman said in a piping treble, "Didn't Mr. Gladstone pray before he went into parliament?"

He covered these points thoroughly but he left out exposition of the social credit gospel.

The platform of the party adopted at Friday afternoon's session is likewise vague on the main points. Plank one proposes "the cessation of borrowing from outside sources and the creation of our own credit" and lets it go at that. A clear cleavage with Major Douglas appears in the plank on the "just price". In the Douglas terminology the "just price" means a price below the cost of production. In the Aberhart economics, as defined by the platform, it means a "fair" price not below cost of production.

If this all sounds rather confusing, it is an accurate report. That was how the convention sounded. The platform was parsed with little debate almost exactly as drawn up by the "central committee", which means Mr. Aberhart.

---

10 STRONG PERSONALITY

By Homer H. Ramage

Edmonton Journal
April 8, 1935

Three years ago a Calgary school teacher came to Edmonton to mark examination papers. In the course of a casual conversation a friend asked him had he heard about the Douglas system and loaned him a book, "Unemployment or War," [by Maurice Colbourne] touching on the theories of Major H.C. Douglas, British engineer and economist and founder of the Social Credit movement.

In this chance occurrence was the seed of a political development that is sweeping Alberta. This Calgary teacher was William Aberhart, Alberta Social Credit leader, probably better known, in the north at least, as the "man who wants to give every adult in Alberta a basic dividend of $25 a month"—the bald finality of which statement, however, Mr. Aberhart points out, has no justification in any statements made by him.

Just a year ago, when Mr. Aberhart was speaking before the provincial legislature, he was referred to vaguely by Edmonton newspapers and the press outside the province as "a Calgary school teacher." Now he probably is the most prominent, if most enigmatic, figure on the Alberta political horizon.

If comparatively unknown until recently outside the sphere of his influence, it must be said that for several years his portly figure has been familiar to thousands more in the southern part of Alberta.

A handsome brown brick building on the main street of Calgary, with a huge jutting sign reading: "Calgary Prophetic Bible Institute," close to the heart of the foothills city, stands as a monument to the ability of Mr. Aberhart as a leader and his genius as an organizer and orator.

He is dean of the Institute, an incorporated company that owns and controls this $65,000 building and has other valuable interests. It is no secret that Mr. Aberhart is the power of this organization.

In appearance and platform manner, Mr. Aberhart has a slight resemblance to Premier Bennett. Slightly taller than average, he is thick set and well dressed. The quizzical blue eyes of a typical school teacher—many Calgary citizens call Mr. Aberhart the best school teacher in Calgary—sparkle behind pince nez glasses, edged in this tortoise-shell and fastened to one ear with a fine gold chain. He is bald with a fringe of white hair.

This is the man, judging from many reports, a great many Albertans [*sic*] want as the next premier of Alberta—a premier who will give them a "new deal." This is the man who is the target of fiery attack from the platform and over the radio by his political foes who are, by no means, concentrated in the north.

Before the writer met Mr. Aberhart, he was told by a Calgary observer: "Aberhart is in the position of a man who rides a tiger; he dare not dismount. He built up a tremendous following in the south with his religious talks and Bible Institute and when he swung into the political field he had no idea the thing would go as far as it has. I think he is sincere enough but I believe he would like very much to get out of it and let others carry through the ideas he believes in. But will his followers let him? Who will take his place?"

Later contact with Mr. Aberhart did not, in the mind of the writer at least, entirely confirm this independent opinion of Mr. Aberhart. The latter did not act like one who was anxious to get out of a movement he had started, for personal convenience, although he did confirm a previous statement that he was not anxious to become premier of Alberta.

Political foes of Mr. Aberhart criticize him for imparting too much of a religious flavor to his political talks and say that Social Credit meetings depend upon religious hysteria to a marked degree.

It is quite true that the Social Credit-ers call Mr. Aberhart a "man of God" and sing rousing political campaign songs that smack strongly of hymns.

The writer dropped into a meeting of a Social Credit group in Calgary—1,500 persons packed into a dance hall—which opened with "O God Our Help in Ages Past"!

The chairman wore the sober blue serge suit of a church deacon, five buttons on the coat, and said he was very proud to be "part of Mr. Aberhart's shadow." When Mr. Aberhart arrived, a 10-piece orchestra was playing loudly but its notes were drowned out by the deafening applause as the crowd caught sight of their leader.

Clearly he is a hero to thousands who may not understand Social Credit but are perfectly willing to have him lead them to a "Promised Land." An ex-newspaperman, now connected with the Social Credit-ers recently wrote: "He is a godly man, skilled in learning, able of mind, clear of vision and, which is more, sincere of purpose, giving, as he sees it, a new message of hope—Social Credit."

As to Mr. Aberhart's talks being flavored with religion—is it not inevitable considering his background? It would be surprising if it were otherwise.

Born in Huron County, Ontario, in 1878, Mr. Aberhart hoped as a youth to train for the ministry. Instead he became a teacher, taking classes at Brantford, Ont., from 1900 to 1910. He received a specialist's certificate in commercial teaching after going through Seaforth collegiate, Queen's University and Hamilton Normal College.

He thought the west offered wider opportunities so in 1910 he arrived at Calgary and became principal of Alexandra public school.

He did not lose his desire to be an instructor in religion through his daily task of teaching the more material subjects.

On his arrival in Calgary he took a Bible class at Trinity church. Later he taught a Bible class in Grace Presbyterian church. In 1912 he joined the Baptist church and organized a Bible class. Here he found scope for his organizing and teaching ability.

With some 60 members, the class started to hold Sunday meetings in a small room of the public library. The class grew rapidly and more space became necessary. It moved to the church auditorium but soon this hall could not accommodate the crowds.

The Grand theatre was rented each Sunday and, Sunday after Sunday, was packed to the doors, persons motoring from points up to 50 miles away to attend the meetings. In 1923 it was necessary to move to the Palace theatre where there was larger seating accommodation and in 1927 the present Calgary Prophetic Bible Institute was built.

Before 1925, radio was still in its infancy, as far as home use was concerned, but in the picture of citizens tinkering with crystal sets, ear phones clamped over their heads to hear this new marvel of science, Mr. Aberhart quickly saw a new avenue of influence. He decided to broadcast his Sunday afternoon lectures on Bible prophecy. It was an instant success.

A Sunday school correspondence department was inaugurated, in connection with the Institute, and now 5,000 boys, girls, young men and young women receive regular lessons by mail, answering questions in the manner of a modern education extension department.

For 20 years now, Mr. Aberhart has been principal of Crescent Heights high school and hundreds of Calgary citizens, engaged in various walks of life, know him as their "old high school principal."

It was not without difficulty that the writer arranged an interview with him. First approached, Mr. Aberhart was sorry but it was impossible to give an interview. Every minute of every day was taken. No, he was not looking for publicity just then. In addition to his school work he was speaking every day, sometimes two or three times a day, and had still more duties to attend to in the way of organization work, preparation for the Social Credit convention, etc.

There was something on his mind that was giving him considerable concern—whether or not to accept the invitation of the legislature to prepare a plan of social credit for Alberta.

It was late one night when the writer "cornered" Mr. Aberhart after he had addressed a big meeting.

Clearly Mr. Aberhart was suffering from the strain of overwork, but with a smile, he consented to answer questions, as best he could. He emphasizes that he has, so far, only laid down general principles. The details he has left to be worked out expertly. He says the government is woefully lacking in statistics that must be secured before any social credit plan could be put into operation.

"My political opponents insist that I stick to my $25 a month. They won't let me budge from this although it was only a suggestion. However I haven't taken it back yet," Mr. Aberhart smiled ....

If the Social Credit party is returned to power at the provincial general election this year, what preliminary steps would be taken to inaugurate social credit in Alberta?, I asked.

"There would need to be a very careful investigation. We would have to build our structure on a firm foundation."

"In this event, how long after the election would you start issuing basic dividends of whatever amount was determined?"

"Between 10 and 15 months, I estimate," Mr. Aberhart answered.

"Who would qualify to receive basic dividends and how many years residence would be required?"

"Bona fide citizens of 21 years or more. We would have to study very carefully the question of qualifications, years of residence and so on."

"What steps would be taken to prevent indigent outsiders from flocking to Alberta in the hope of receiving basic dividends?" I continued.

"Due warning would be given that there would be no dividends for outsiders or transients. Furthermore, no relief would be given."

"Would not your proposed central credit house for clearing non-negotiable basic dividends, certificates and transferring credit from one person to another tend to slow up business greatly?" I asked.

"I do not think so. Branches of the state credit house would be established at every point necessary. Business would be carried on much the same as now."

"The great bulk of commodities sold in Alberta are produced outside the province. How would wholesalers manage to pay for them, it being assumed that Alberta social credit certificates would be of no value outside the province?"

"When a wholesaler pays an account outside the province, no actual money is transferred now."

"Yes, that is quite true," I said. "When a person in Alberta pays an account in another province, or another country, no actual money is transferred. However, would the creditor in another country or province accept drafts or money orders issued by the Alberta state credit house? What tangible backing would there be to assure their free acceptance outside the province?"

"The state credit house would issue only dominion money orders. There would be the backing of the natural resources of the province, the second richest province in Canada. Social Credit simply is a scientific means of distribution within the province. There are angles to this question that need further consideration. I would not care to attempt an answer any more comprehensive at this time," Mr. Aberhart said.

---

11 WHERE IS MONEY TO COME FROM?

Calgary Herald
April 9, 1935

There is before the people of Alberta today a proposed plan for the distribution of non-negotiable certificates by the province, which can be used for the purchase of commodities and the settlement of personal debts. If the idea is understood correctly, these certificates will perform all the functions which Dominion currency and bank bills do at the present time. They will be legal tender within the province.

What a great many people want to know is what the basis of backing will be as a foundation for their value. The proponents of the plan have stated that such backing will consist of the productive wealth and natural resources of Alberta, but unless the plan means downright confiscation of production, together with the placing of an arbitrary value upon natural resources, it is impossible to see how such a plan could be economically sound.

And for the following reasons. Money is not real wealth, it is capital. Real wealth consists of labor, resources and the machinery of production. Natural resources are not real wealth, but simply potential wealth. The application of labour to natural resources produces real wealth when capital is applied to the process.

In order to create credit—and it is a non-negotiable credit instrument that is being discussed—there must be a capital foundation. This foundation must consist of negotiable instruments, or titles to wealth. Upon this basis credit can be issued, and it does not make the slightest bit of difference whether it is done through the medium of a bank or a state credit house, every such credit item issued must return intact to its source.

The plan proposed is supposed to work in a capitalistic economy, but it is impossible to see how it will work satisfactorily unless it has a base in negotiable wealth. Where is this to come from unless it proceeds from outright confiscation? The difficulties in the way of this course would be enormous. On the other hand, if it is proposed simply to print certificates or even to deposit credit to individual accounts in the state credit house, such a plan would be straight inflation. The redemption of such certificates could only be achieved through the medium of taxation. It is reasonable to assert that the province could not redeem any greater amount of such certificates than the total of the revenue collected through taxation.

---

12 DELIBERATE DECEPTION

Edmonton Bulletin
April 12, 1935

Major Douglas has been engaged by the Government of Alberta, under a two-year contract, to formulate a Social Credit system applicable to Alberta, the expense involved to be met out of the public funds, including no doubt a suitable honorarium for the time spent and service rendered.

But Ex-Premier Brownlee goes on the air to proclaim that the legislature of Alberta has no constitutional right to introduce any kind of a Social Credit system, and no power to enforce compliance with such a system if one were attempted.

Not a word has come from Attorney General Lymburn, flanked by a dozen departmental lawyers, to suggest that the legislature has any such power. It is fair to assume that Mr. Brownlee speaks the opinion of the Government of which he was lately the head, when he says the legislature holds no authority to introduce a Social Credit plan or to apply measures for its enforcement. In the silence of Mr. Lymburn and all the other Ministers on the subject, such must be taken to be the fact.

Where then are we "at" in this matter of Social Credit? Two men have been employed, or invited, to prepare and present plans to do something which the ex-Premier, and present spokesman of the Government, says the legislature has no power to do. Public money is to be spent for an object which is declared by him to be illegal. One man is being brought across the Atlantic and a resident of this province is asked to spend time and effort, for a purpose of which Mr. Brownlee says nothing can come.

Once again: Is the Government trifling with Major Douglas, with Mr. Aberhart, and with the taxpayers of the province? What other construction can be placed upon this exhibition of bare-faced duplicity?

Not a member of the Government has professed to believe the legislature can set up a Social Credit system of any kind. Mr. Brownlee apparently speaking for the Government, and the only man undertaking to do so from the constitutional point of view, says in most definite terms that the legislature cannot do anything of the kind. Yet Major Douglas has been hired, and Mr. Aberhart is invited to submit plans for Social Credit systems to be put into operation in the province by authority of the provincial legislature.

Whatever the Government may think of Social Credit, the advocates of that theory and the taxpayers of the province are alike and at least entitled to be dealt with candidly. That is not the kind of treatment they are getting. Taxpayer money is to be spent, and the time of Major Douglas and Mr. Aberhart wasted in devising schemes which the exponent of the Government's legal opinions declares to be impossible of adoption.

There is only one term applicable to this course of double-dealing. It is a strategy of calculated deception.

13 ABERHART SPEAKS IN EDMONTON

Calgary Albertan
April 23, 1935

More than 7,000 persons tonight heard William Aberhart, Alberta social credit leader from Calgary, declare, "I'm the Pied Piper from Hamlin" and that he liked this characterization, given to him "because the Pied Piper drove the rats out of the capital city."

The crowd was a capacity house for the city-owned arena.

Mr. Aberhart declared that he had not made a social credit plan for Alberta because he first wanted the people of the province to understand at what he was aiming. Apparently referring to the provincial government's invitation to address the Legislature and present a plan, which he declined, he said, "I will not be forced forward faster than it can be done."

Answering critics who said that taxation would grow under social credit, Mr. Aberhart declared "We can reduce taxation as we go along" and that under social credit, "we will float out to the place where taxes will become less and less."

He denied that the payments of what he described as basic dividends to the bona fide residents of Alberta would make them "a bunch of lazy loafers" and suggested that those who have earned dividends in the past on investments they had made did not make them on this type.

He deprecated "mud-slinging" and deplored that "we can't discuss things quietly and earnestly seek a way out of our present troubles without a man's character being inquired into to the third or fourth generation back."

A band played while the audience sang "O God Our Help in Ages Past" and Mr. Aberhart said "I believe that Christian men and women will go forward and say we must have a new order."

The social credit leader found that there is no other outlet for school graduates today than "those miserable camps" and promised that under his system there would be better things for them.

14 ABERHART INVOKES BOYCOTT

Calgary Herald
April 29, 1935

If anything further were needed to convince the people of Alberta that a new and highly dangerous type of political leadership has put in its appearance in this province, the radio address of William Aberhart, leader of the new social credit party, on Sunday afternoon from the pulpit of the Prophetic Bible Institute will supply it.

He advised all his followers to boycott the Calgary Herald for "the next few months" because, he said, this newspaper is unfair to him. It is difficult to discover in what way the Herald has been "unfair" to him unless it is that we have dared to counsel the people of this province to beware of the will-of-the-wisp promises that this pulpiteer is dangling before them. We have pointed out the financial and constitutional weaknesses of his plan as far as he has divulged it, as is the duty of a newspaper. At the same time we have given generous space to the expression of views favorable to the Aberhart plan.

Surely it is very surprising to find the leader of a Christian movement and the head of a political party inviting his followers to injure an established industry which employs a large number of citizens. These employees of the Herald have contributed largely in the past and still do to the payment of Mr. Aberhart's salary as principal of the Crescent Heights High School.

Is everyone opposed to the political opinions and plans of Mr. Aberhart to be boycotted? He has invoked a most dangerous precedent and has given the people of this province a foretaste of the Hitlerism which will prevail if he ever secures control of the provincial administration.

15 CULTS, ISMS OF WEST IRK HANSON

Edmonton Bulletin
May 1, 1935

"I am amazed since out west at the number of cults and isms creeping up on the political horizon," declared Hon. R.B. Hanson, [Conservative] Minister of Trade and Commerce, Tuesday at a Board of Trade dinner here.

Referring specifically to the Social Credit theory now rampant in Alberta, Mr. Hanson said, "The theory is running through whole communities like a mess of weasels." He forecast disillusionment to many in Alberta if the Social Creditors "unfortunately win the provincial election". Mr. Hanson also warned Saskatchewan against Social Credit.

Mr. Hanson referred to suggested alternatives to capitalism. Speaking of Social Credit, he said, "I know Mr. Douglas. He was paid fat fees to tell us (at Ottawa) something we couldn't understand."

Mr. Hanson saw the Aberhart theory of Social Credit as being preached in Alberta as "different from Douglas."

"I asked Bill Irvine, (U.F.A. member for Wetaskiwin) what the theory was," Mr. Hanson said. "Mr. Irvine said it was Douglas on one hand and the Holy Ghost on the other."

16 ALBERTA FACES STRANGE ELECTION

Calgary Herald
July 17, 1935

The Reid Government has decided to make the plunge. The provincial election date has been set for August 22, and the province faces one of the most complicated campaigns in its history. In addition to the Liberals, Conservatives, U.F.A., and Labor, the four main parties in past campaigns, there will be candidates representing Aberhart social credit, Communism, Douglas social credit, socialism, and what not. Anything may emerge from a melee of the kind and at present the popular assumption is that no one group will attain a working majority.

This entrance of the Aberhart social credit party into the fray adds to the uncertainty of the polling. Its leader proposes to place candidates in every riding but has indicated more than once that he will not contest a seat himself. This decision may bring him some advantages, obviating for one thing the risk of personal defeat, but it is an extraordinary course for a party leader to pursue. Competent observers declare that the social credit campaign is losing ground, largely because of growing realization among the farmers that the Aberhart proposals, if put into effect, would bear most heavily upon them as a class. Inability to present a coherent plan and a constant contradiction of previous statements are also proving unfortunate for the new political party's success at the polls. However, it is still too soon to predict with any accuracy to what extent the Aberhartists will cut into the normal following of other parties.

It must be obvious to the Government by this time that it made a tactical blunder in holding on to office so long. An election a year ago would have avoided certain conditions which are proving uncomfortable today. The delay has given the Aberhart movement a chance to pursue a year's intensive campaigning over the radio and at public meetings and to acquire a political prominence which its platform and its absurd promises do not warrant. There were, however, reasons which the Reid Government no doubt thought sufficient to justify holding on to office another year. Its followers in the legislature were not keen to forego another assured sessional indemnity in a time of depression, and certain unsavory court cases in which prominent members of the government were involved were also a factor in suggesting a delayed appeal to the people. It was no doubt felt that public memory is proverbially short and that election post-ponement for a year might contribute to the reinstatement in favor of those party stalwarts.

Apart from the new political movement, the U.F.A. administration faces other difficulties which were not acute in 1930. At that time the effects of the depression were barely observable. There was no unemployment problem of any dimension, and further governmental borrowing was not such an acute problem as it is today. Farmers and other classes of the community thought then that the depression would be short-lived, and the critical spirit that has since developed against any and all governments was not in evidence. Today the government is seeking a renewal of its mandate under a new and comparatively untried leader, with few legislative or constructive plans of any kind designed to improve conditions during the past five years to its credit. It has been in office since 1921 and in that time has added enormously to the public debt. There is a feeling that the cabinet have exhausted their administrative usefulness. The cry for a change is always most acute in hard times and so far government spokesmen have not been particularly effective in convincing the electors that they are entitled to another four—or will it be five?—years in office.

The Herald believes that in view of the critical situation in which the province finds itself, and the possible danger through the presence in the field of so many groups that a highly fantastic economic program might win serious support, there should have been a working agreement among the groups opposed to Aberhart social credit. However, the Liberal leader, with his mind, no doubt, on Liberal successes in other provinces, has refused to consider anything in the way of a coalition campaign, and the merry free-for-all is on. As the campaign will be conducted, it will not be possible for opponents of social credit, and they are in a great majority, to make their votes solidly effective against a common enemy. Their support will be split up among several parties, while social creditors will vote as a solid unit.

17 SOCIAL CREDIT CANDIDATES NAMED

Calgary Herald
July 23, 1935

Sixty-three Social Credit candidates have been selected by Mr. Aberhart and his advisory committee to contest every seat in the province. The leader himself is remaining on the side lines, but he has sent nearly all his leading organizers into the fray. It is obvious from the line-up finally chosen that the seeds of dissension have been sown. In the Calgary approved list are at least two men who were not chosen by the nominating convention.

Apparently they were a personal choice of the inner circle.

A feature of the list is the great number of professional men chosen for rural ridings. There are many doctors, teachers, preachers and lawyers, but a dearth of practical farmers. Only twelve of the latter are listed among the sixty-three, which is an extraordinary small number for a province predominantly devoted to agriculture.

The method of selecting candidates adopted by the Social Credit party, by which four men were selected by Popular choice in each riding with Mr. Aberhart himself making the final choice out of this number, is an extraordinary one. No political leader within memory in a democratic country has ever attempted to put any similar plan into effect. The object, of course, is apparent. It places the nominees under the personal dictation of the party leader and gives him autocratic control of the party. It places a premium on yes-men, and the selection of so many lieutenants of Mr. Aberhart with consequent rejection, of practical farmers and others wanted in the constituencies indicates the arbitrary temper of the party leader. On the other hand, it is bound to create a great deal of bad feeling among the friends of the rejected convention nominees, especially as in the case in this city, the leader and his advisory council have gone outside the official list of nominees to select men who may have some special claim to their consideration. It is thus obvious the will of the people means little to men of autocratic leanings enjoying temporary power.

18 FORETASTE OF WHAT WILL HAPPEN

Edmonton Journal
July 24, 1935

An Edmonton merchant informs the Journal that he has just received a letter from an English business house, with which he has dealt for twelve years, that reads: "We regret to state that owing to recent happenings in your province we must ask that from and after August 1 your orders shall be accompanied by a remittance to cover the amount of your order." This he regards as a foretaste of what will happen to Alberta business concerns if "fantastic and impossible proposals" now being advocated receive the endorsation of the electors of the province. Confidence in their credit, on the part of those with whom they have had trade relations, having already been impaired, the writer of the letter looks for it to be entirely destroyed if the Aberhart campaign should succeed.

There is plenty of other evidence of the alarm that is being felt not only throughout Canada, but in other countries as well over the political possibilities in Alberta. It has been impressed on many in all lines of activity besides the merchant who supplies this information. The apparent strength of the social credit agitation has led to the postponement of enterprises which, if undertaken this summer, would have eased unemployment and stimulated general recovery. It is essential if confidence is to be restored and the wheels of progress set going again that the social credit proposals be decisively rejected next month. They are of such a nature as to demand that they be fought with the utmost vigor. Anyone who, while realizing on what an unsound basis they rest, gives encouragement to their advocates in order to serve an immediate political or personal purpose shows a poor sense of his public duty.

19 SOCIAL CREDITORS LACKING IN HUMOUR

Calgary Herald
July 26, 1935

As the present political campaign in Alberta develops, it is becoming increasingly apparent that the followers of Mr. Aberhart lack a saving sense of humor and tolerance toward opposing opinions. The boycott, threats and innuendoes are becoming their stock reply to those who venture to suggest that the social credit claims are fantastic and that the Aberhart plan cannot be put into effect in this province without disastrous consequences. This is an extraordinary manifestation on the part of a political party which originated under religious auspices and which broadcasts most of its leading propaganda from a pulpit every Sunday. The general public had a right to expect, under these circumstances, charity to opponents and tolerance to opposing opinions, but these qualities are conspicuous by their absence.

The leader of the new party has complained on numerous occasions against "the mudslinging tactics" of his opponents. But he himself set an example—not generally followed, fortunately—by referring to the U.F.W.A. as the "Undernourished Fool Women of Alberta". It is said that he has expressed regret for this slur, but the example thus set has been adopted by one of his candidates in Calgary. She has referred to the Economic Safety League, a group which includes in its membership many estimable fellow-citizens as the "Elevated Society of Lunatics". Evidently the general public may expect more of this typical brand of social credit wit—or is it mudslinging?

The Herald is not escaping, along with many others who see fit to criticize the Aberhart proposals, the fulminations that social creditors cast at critics. Two typical communications arrived in yesterday's mail. "A True Social Creditor"—the usual anonymous signature—wrote: "From now on you can keep your paper of lies and tommyrot to yourself for we wouldn't have such a paper in the house, and I hope a good many more will do the same". Thus is expressed the usual social credit wish to see opponents suffer monetary or other misfortunes.

Another confirmed social credit disciple from the interior of the province writes in similar uncharitable vein, but he goes farther by denying the right of comment on public developments to the daily press. He says: "While I have resented your editorial page for a long time, your nasty, dirty and unfair editorials in connection with the social credit party's method of selecting their candidates are entirely out of place and uncalled for from you, as I consider that it is absolutely none of your business".

It would seem that such a radical departure in the selection of party candidates IS a matter of public interest and therefore open to comment. If the system were adopted by the other parties, free choice by constituents of their representatives would soon be a thing of the past.

Well, it is a good thing the campaign will soon be over, and the mudslinging and lack of humor and lack of tolerance will be things of the past. The people have no reason to be proud of the prejudice and the intolerance in evidence at this time, which fortunately, did not exist in past campaigns. The responsibility for the present type of campaign cannot be evaded by the leader of the Social Credit party.

20 CALGARY BOARD OF TRADE AND SOCIAL CREDIT

Calgary Herald
August 8, 1935

It having been represented to the Calgary Board of Trade that people were looking to it for some statement regarding Social Credit, the Council of the Board, after very prolonged and careful consideration of the arguments for and against the proposals, has decided to submit the following as its considered conclusions on the subject:—

1. The proposals must necessarily involve crushing taxation entirely beyond the capacity of the people of Alberta to pay.

2. Any attempt to fix just prices can only result in incredible confusion and paralysis of business to the detriment of every producer and consumer.

3. The suggestion that dividends can be paid out of cultural heritage and undeveloped natural resources is impracticable and impossible.

4. The Social Credit monetary proposals will lead to a condition similar to that which occurred in Germany, involving the Province, the farmer, the wage earner, etc., in financial disaster.

5. The Social Credit proposals will isolate Alberta and render it impossible for either the farmer or the business man to buy or sell to advantage.

6. Finally, such an experiment as is outlined by the Social Credit proposals will lead to chaos, and entail great suffering, from which the Province would not recover for many years.

Inserted by the ECONOMIC SAFETY
LEAGUE, CALGARY

| Hon. Dr. W. Egbert | Jesse Gouge |
| President | Secretary |

21 CHAMBER'S IMPRESSIVE WARNING

Edmonton Journal
August 8, 1935

In expressing its opinions regarding the social credit proposals, the Edmonton Chamber of Commerce has taken an unusual step for such a body. It has hitherto stood aside from political issues but feels that it would be failing in its duty if it did not point out how serious would be the consequences if the electors should endorse Mr. Aberhart's ideas. The chamber is fully justified in thus departing from the rule to which it has rigidly adhered in the past. It could not be silent when the whole economic life of the province is exposed to so grave a threat.

The unsoundness of the proposals has never been more clearly demonstrated than in the address which the secretary-manager, Mr. Blue, delivered on Tuesday evening. Mr. Aberhart was given credit for the best of motives, while the zeal and ability that he has brought to the advocacy of his cause were recognized. It was insisted, however, that the qualities which have induced so many to give him their support merely increased his responsibility. This is something of which he has not shown himself sufficiently mindful. Certainly he is not entitled to receive the mandate that he seeks simply because he possesses these qualities, when it has been shown beyond any shadow of doubt that his policies are founded on complete economic fallacies and that their adoption would lead to an intensification of the difficulties and hardships that Alberta has already experienced.

Mr. Blue set forth in detail the many reasons why the chamber is so much concerned over the possibility that Mr. Aberhart will be placed in control of the legislature and thus be enabled to make the attempt to put his plan into effect. Their validity ought to be apparent to all who examine them with an open mind.

It is a straight appeal to the intelligence of the citizens that the chamber has made. It only asks that criticism it offers of the social credit proposals be considered on its merits and that they pay due regard to their individual interests, as well as those of the province as a whole, that are at stake. An organization that has given the public such good service over a long period of years and has at all times manifested so high a sense of its responsibility deserves to have the closest attention paid by every elector to the warning it has issued.

22 THE ONE WAY OUT — A LIBERAL VIEW

Edmonton Bulletin
August 14, 1935

The Edmonton Bulletin, long before Mr. Aberhart's scheme of Social Credit was heard about, blazed the way to public enlightenment on the inequalities and rank injustices that exist in this age of plenty.

That thousands are denied the necessities of life, that our young men are herded into semi-military camps, that business men are being driven to the wall, homes seized and hope denied our citizens, are themes dwelt upon by The Bulletin, with all possible force and plain-speaking. It has dared, time and again, to challenge the money-powers and special privileged interests responsible for our present bondage.

Surely, then, The Bulletin is justified in speaking its mind openly and opposing, with all the strength at its command, what it considers to be a movement which threatens the very existence of what little economic stability is still left to us.

Mr. Aberhart finds no foe in The Bulletin when he denounces economic abuses. Without the missionary work done by this paper, his indictment of the financial powers responsible for our predicament would have fallen with much less effect on the public ear. Everything he says along these lines has been said a hundred times in the past few years by this paper.

The issue does not lie in this quarter. The issue between The Bulletin and Mr. Aberhart hinges on the question of the best way to eliminate these abuses. The Bulletin believes that Mr. Aberhart's "way out" is, actually, a "way in" to greater distress, by far, than any we have yet experienced. It is satisfied that confusion, chaos and even deeper suffering, combined with bitter disillusionment and despair, lie ahead of [sic] Albertans if they vote for Mr. Aberhart's Social Credit candidates.

The only possible way to change conditions and get immediate results is to vote for Liberal candidates and elect a Liberal government. All other provinces are now Liberal and Alberta has the chance of a lifetime to play an important part in the coming conferences which will deal with the necessary changes in the B.N.A. Act and may radically change duties and responsibilities of the Dominion, Provincial and Municipal governments.

By working in close co-operation with the incoming Liberal government at Ottawa, Alberta can and will get a NEW START and a NEW DEAL.

Think it over!

23 IF ABERHART SHOULD WIN

Edmonton Journal
August 15, 1935

You hear men and women say, "Oh, I think I'll vote Social Credit. That $25 a month will come in mighty handy. And if Aberhart cannot make it stick and I don't get the twenty-five, well, I'll be no worse off than I am now. Things can't get worse."

BUT—things CAN get worse in Alberta—much worse.

There is strong evidence to indicate that if a Social Credit government were elected next Thursday, things would get very much worse in Alberta.

And the people who would suffer most are the so-called "little fellows." Those with money could, and many would, move out. But the little fellows, the wage earners, the small-salaried men, the chaps who have put their all in a little home and could not get away—all these will have to stay here and take it.

Why does the Journal put it in this blunt way? Because it has learned of some things that have convinced it beyond any possibility of doubt that conditions would be infinitely worse in Alberta if a Social Credit government were elected.

The time has come to tell these things, so that the little fellows may vote to protect their jobs, their wages, their homes.

The Journal knows that one large commercial house has already made preparations to move, bag and baggage, to a neighboring province, if on August 23 it is clear that Alberta has gone in for a Social Credit experiment.

Think what that will mean to the employees of this firm. Many of them will not be able to pull up stakes and move with the company. They will have to stay and "take it." They will lose their jobs at a time when jobs are so very hard to find. And many of them will, as a consequence, lose their homes, too.

Truckers and railway men will suffer also, for this firm will then be shipping its goods from some city outside Alberta and workers in that city will gain what these Alberta workers will lose.

The Journal knows that one big firm, which is ready and anxious to open up for business in Alberta, is waiting until election day is over before going on with its plans. It is ready to spend hundreds of thousands of dollars in Alberta within the next year, putting up buildings, buying equipment, and so on. But not if Social Credit carries. If Alberta goes Social Credit, this big concern will not come into Alberta, at least not for years—and perhaps never if in the meantime it should set up its western centre of operations in some other province.

Think what this will mean to laborers, to skilled artisans, to clerks, to stenographers, to a whole host of people who would get jobs with this concern if it should open up in Alberta. No such jobs for them if Social Credit carries!

The Journal knows that men and women who have money lying idle in Alberta are waiting for election day to decide whether they will put that money to work here, or will take it away to some other province.

Think what a "flight of the dollar" from Alberta would mean to carpenters, bricklayers, stone masons, steam-fitters, electricians and to a host of other artisans and laborers. Hundreds of homes are waiting to be built in Alberta. The men who could finance their building have been waiting to see how the people of Alberta vote next Thursday.

The Journal knows that Alberta would have been enjoying a mild building boom right now if it had not been for the threat of Social Credit. If that threat is turned into fact, it will be years before trust companies, mortgage companies and individual men and women who have money to invest will put a cent of it into Alberta.

Think what stagnation of the building industry has meant already. Think how it will affect thousands of wage earners if it continues for another eighteen months or two years while a Social Credit government is trying to launch its proposed system. Mr. Aberhart himself says it will take that long to work out details of his plan.

Two years of depressed business, of lower wages, of fewer jobs. And there's no telling how much longer!

No wonder the Labor party, as the representative of organized wage earners, is fighting Social Credit so strongly.

Things will indeed be worse—much worse—if Social Credit carries next Thursday. And it is not the rich who will suffer most. Many of them will pack up and get out! It is the wage earners, the little fellows who cannot get away who will bear the brunt. And the farmers will share their full measure.

Mr. Aberhart apparently is quite willing to experiment with the men, women and children of Alberta "for the good of humanity," in spite of the fact that Major Douglas, whose disciple Mr. Aberhart claims to be, has stated emphatically that Social Credit should be attempted only on a national scale. The people of Alberta have had enough of experiments—of low wages, scarce jobs and living on the dole. They do not want another two years more of it—just to give Mr. Aberhart an opportunity to turn Alberta into an economic test tube in which they would be the unhappy amalgam to be subjected to the corrosive acid of unsound experiment.

24 REASONS TO VOTE FOR SOCIAL CREDIT

Alberta Social Credit Chronicle
August 16, 1935

1. SOCIAL CREDIT means freedom.
2. SOCIAL CREDIT takes nothing from you; It Gives.
3. SOCIAL CREDIT believes in education not compulsion.
4. SOCIAL CREDIT stands for entire freedom of religious belief.

5. SOCIAL CREDIT believes in better legislation.
6. SOCIAL CREDIT means "Government of the people, by the people and for the people."
7. SOCIAL CREDIT will not interfere with your pensions in any way.
8. SOCIAL CREDIT will not interfere with your Savings in any way.
9. SOCIAL CREDIT will not interfere with your insurance. Relief will not be interfered with, except for improvements, until basic dividends are issued.
10. SOCIAL CREDIT means reduction in taxes.
11. SOCIAL CREDIT means help and protection to the individual producer.
12. SOCIAL CREDIT believes that the liquor question should be solved by education not legislation.
13. SOCIAL CREDIT will create employment.
14. SOCIAL CREDIT permits you to will money or property to whomsoever you wish.
15. SOCIAL CREDIT believes that the aged or unfit should not have to work to live.
16. SOCIAL CREDIT believes that special allowances must be made, in addition to basic dividends, for large families of children.
17. SOCIAL CREDIT dividends would enable elderly People to retire, making way for youth.
18. SOCIAL CREDIT permits citizens, wishing to visit another province or country to convert their basic dividend into currency before leaving Alberta.

25 ABERHART AND THE ELECTION

Edmonton Journal
August 16, 1935

Alberta has the eyes of the world upon it and is getting more publicity than it ever had before, said William Aberhart, Social Credit leader, at a Westmount meeting Thursday.

Not only in the other provinces of Canada but in many states across the line, and in Australia, England, Denmark, and other countries, declared Mr. Aberhart, Alberta is being watched for the outcome of next week's elections, and it now has an opportunity to "lead the world along the path of progress."

Westmount community hall was fairly well filled, obviously with Social Credit sympathizers, and when a standing vote of S.C. supporters was taken, at the leader's request, it was nearly unanimous.

Complaints against the other parties for the methods adopted by them in opposition to Social Credit featured the addresses of Mr. Aberhart and five candidates who also were on the program.

Again asserting that full information about Social Credit details is not necessary for voters, Mr. Aberhart told his audience that experts would put the scheme into operation if only the people cast their ballots in the right way. If they were not afterward satisfied with the results, he said, they could recall, a provision not included in the platform of any other party.

"Be sure you vote 1-2-3-4-5-6 for the Social Credit candidates," urged Mr. Aberhart, "and go on after that if you can stand it. I don't care much whether you do or not."

"Monetary reform as now being talked by the opposition is an Ottawa matter," Mr. Aberhart observed, "and it will take 15 years to get action in that quarter. We can't wait that long, and now is the opportunity for Alberta to lead Canada if you have the judgment to vote for Social Credit."

Mr. Aberhart characterized the criticisms of the old-line parties as lies and misrepresentations, spread through the country in the hope of making a cleavage among the people and introducing race prejudice. He repeated his denials of various rumors about himself, declared that the talk about confiscating railway cheques was "bunk," and noted the fact that practically the whole press of Alberta was opposed to Social Credit.

It having been suggested by one of the candidates that Mr. Aberhart would be the next premier, he said he would be "delighted if the time ever comes to be asked to come to Edmonton to live."

26 SOCIAL CREDIT WINS ELECTION

Calgary Herald
August 23, 1935

Alberta will have a Social Credit government, headed by William Aberhart, the 57-year-old Calgary founder of the Alberta Social Credit League.

In its initial bid for power, and the first time the electors of a Canadian province have ever been offered a social credit administration, the league candidates made a sweep of the rural ridings. They were also among the leaders as the proportional representation count proceeded at an early hour this morning in the cities.

Premier Reid, head of the U.F.A. government since 1934, when he succeeded Hon. J.E. Brownlee in the premiership, was defeated by social credit in his riding of Vermilion. He has represented Vermilion in the legislature since 1921, the year the U.F.A. defeated the Liberal regime which had held power from the formation of the province in 1905.

All the Reid cabinet members were defeated, or far behind their opponents, with the exception of Hon. J.F. Lymburn, attorney-general, who was running fifth in the six-seat Edmonton constituency in the second count here.

W.R. Howson, the Liberal leader, was re-elected on the first choice count in Edmonton, while John Irwin, veteran Calgary member, was the only Conservative in the province to be elected at press time.

Hon. J.E. Brownlee, former premier who was running for re-election in Ponoka, was defeated by his Social Credit opponent, Mrs. W.W. Rogers, one of the leaders in the new movement.

The Social Credit men made a clean sweep in the southern rural constituencies. In the single member ridings of Medicine Hat and Lethbridge, Liberal and Labor stalwarts, members of the last legislature, lost. In the north, Liberals and the U.F.A. candidates suffered the heavy defeat.

E.C. Manning, chief aide of Mr. Aberhart in sponsoring the new economic plan, headed the Calgary poll.

In Drumheller, centre of a coal mining district, F.G. Moyer, Independent party leader in the last legislature, was swept out of office by H. Ingrey, the Social Credit candidate. Murdoch Clarke, well known Alberta Communist, failed at his attempt to gain election in Drumheller as did Duncan McDonald, Liberal.

O.L. McPherson, former minister of public works, who represented Little Bow riding in the legislature, was forced out of office. Rev. Peter Dawson, the Social Credit nominee, was the victor. The defeated included L.H. Stack, Liberal.

Surrounded by members of the Social Credit League in Calgary, Mr. Aberhart, who was not a candidate, received the election returns at the Prophetic Bible Institute, which he founded in Calgary some years ago. It was here he organized the Social Credit League.

27 ABERHART DENIES CONFISCATION CHARGE

Edmonton Bulletin
August 24, 1935

Declaring integrity of the province would be maintained, William Aberhart, whose Alberta Social Credit League soared to power in the provincial election, today said investors in Alberta need have no fear of a Social Credit government.

The latest party standing gave the Social Credit forces 45 seats, Liberals four and Conservatives two in the 63-seat house. Social Credit nominees were leading in 12 seats, Liberals in one and United Farmers of Alberta, the previous governing party, leading in one.

Mr. Aberhart's statement, issued to the Canadian Press, said:

"Our money is standing absolutely standard. Social Credit is determined to maintain the credit of the country at par. There is no better investment in Canada than Alberta bonds at the present time. We have no intention of confiscating or repudiation in any way, shape or form."

"Our purpose is simply to scientifically distribute the goods and services we have in abundance. No rash or precipitate action will be considered. We will build on a firm foundation."

28 ABERHART PLEADS FOR SUPPORT

Calgary Herald
September 16, 1935

"You can refuse if you like and see the blood run red down the streets," William Aberhart, Alberta's new premier, told 1,000 of his home-town folks who packed the First Presbyterian church here last night to hear the Social Credit leader make an impassioned plea for their prayers and support in establishing the system which he hopes will abolish poverty in the prairie province.

Appealing for whole-hearted support, "down to the last man and woman in Ontario," the premier said: "You can't take religion to a man who has had nothing to eat for three days and can get nothing for wife and children at home; he won't listen to you. There are people starving in Alberta; there are women in Alberta who have worn nothing but gunny sacks for the past three years, dresses made from the bags in which the binder twine was wrapped."

"There are children in Alberta who have not tasted butter or milk in the last three years although they live on farms. Their fathers have to sell all the milk the cows produce to live."

"I can find no answer to this but the philosophy of social credit. Social credit is applied religion, that is my theory."

"Children are crying for food out in Alberta tonight. The boys and girls are hungry and they are your neighbors. Will Ontario listen? We are asking for your support. We are asking you to pray for us and give us a chance to balance our budgets and don't listen to those who are attempting to destroy our credit before we get started. Give us your co-operation and we will buy goods."

Later the premier motored to Mitchell where he also addressed a church gathering.

On Saturday Mr. Aberhart discussed his program with Rev. Father C.E. Coughlin in Detroit, and after the conference Father Coughlin issued a statement in which he commended the western premier's theories. "Both Premier Aberhart and Alberta are to be congratulated on his forward step," he declared.

The entire population of this town turned out to greet the premier as he arrived from Detroit to spend the week-end with his mother, Mrs. William Aberhart, at the home of his brother, Charles.

Mayor Sutheraind [*sic*] and the town council met him on his arrival and at a civic reception officially welcomed him as "one of Seaforth's sons who has returned with honor and distinction."

"I am mighty glad to be back and hear these kind words," said Premier Aberhart. "It takes me back to the old days when I used to go up from Edmondville to school in Seaforth and play football with Seaforth Hurons. It is a mighty fine thing to be back here and tell you how we have been fighting for the cause of the common people."

"One is impressed in looking around to see the large number of cars and every indication of prosperity. In Alberta they cannot buy cars or gasoline. Conditions in that province almost made me a Communist, although I have no use for Communism. Instead I turn to social credit."

"Alberta is the second richest province in the Dominion per capita, although we have not as large a population as Ontario, and still we have distress and poverty in the midst of plenty. We have an abundance of wheat, coal and natural gas and yet people are starving because we cannot sell them. Let us put purchasing power into the hands of the consumer," he said.

The premier said he hopes to see his mission completed, through the medium of social credit, in five years. Political life, he said, is distasteful to him but not as distasteful as the present state of affairs in Alberta.

Premier Aberhart went back to Toronto Monday in time to attend a private luncheon tendered him by Floyd Chalmers, editor of the Financial Post. He was to leave for the west tonight, stopping off for addresses at Winnipeg on Wednesday and Saskatoon on Thursday.

29 POOR PUBLICITY FOR ALBERTA

Calgary Herald
September 17, 1935

Whatever else he may be the new premier of Alberta is evidently not a good publicity agent to send outside the province which has conferred on him the highest office in its power. Speaking in his old home town in Ontario on Sunday, he is reported as making statements which the great majority of the people of Alberta will regard as extravagant and absurd. Propagandist zeal for a special cause provides no excuse.

"Children are crying for food out in Alberta tonight. The boys and girls are hungry." Thus Mr. Aberhart. If his facts are right, it is not because there has been any stinting in supplies for those in need. Through the three-way system of relief adopted in the urban centres and in the provincial and federal co-operation for the care of single unemployed, there has been in effect for the past few years a plan by which every needy person is given full opportunity to secure public assistance.

For the eight months ending on August 31 last the city of Calgary expended on relief the huge sum of $538,710. In the three months ending June 30 last, the province's net expenditure on relief was $521,172. During the same three months the federal contribution to Alberta relief was $300,000. In view of this large scale expenditure, the taxpayers cannot be accused of neglecting the unfortunates. Neither is it likely, on the same showing, that "many boys and girls in Alberta are going without food."

Mr. Aberhart also declared that in Alberta the people cannot buy cars and gasoline. What are the facts? The number of motor vehicles registered in Alberta last year was 89,-369. The percentage of population owning cars was 11.6 per cent. Similar percentages in Manitoba and Saskatchewan were 9.6 and 9.5. Alberta stood third among all the provinces in this regard. Moreover the sale of new cars in this province in 1935 is, according to motor dealers, away above that of last year.

In 1934 the total provincial revenue was $15,178,607, of which $1,950,349 was in gasoline taxes, and $1,690,340 in registration fees. Car owners paid that year $3,650,689 into the provincial treasury, or 24 per cent of the total revenue.

That does not look as if the people of Alberta are not buying cars and gasoline.

30 BENNETT'S VIEWS ON ABERHART

Edmonton Bulletin
October 4, 1935

Any Canadian who could be "so short-sighted, so disloyal to his own interest, as to believe he can be made rich by the employment of the printing press," might well vote against the government, Prime Minister Bennett declared last night. "For no consideration on earth," he said, "will ever make me party to any act which I know will destroy the credit of our country."

Mr. Bennett was discussing the measures he said had been advanced by some of his political opponents for the improvement of monetary conditions in Canada.

Discussing Liberal leader Mackenzie King, the Prime Minister asked—"Why does he not stand on the bridge of Liberalism and go down with his ship so that his friends may mourn him and his enemies honor him?"

Mr. King's recent promise to negotiate a trade treaty with United States, "after nine years in office when he did nothing," was described by the Prime Minister as a "last desperate throw of a desperate politician."

"Mr. King has one policy," the Prime Minister declared, "and that is to defeat a government."

"And we're going to do it," shouted the lone heckler.

"Not you," replied the Prime Minister. "There are too many sensible people in this country."

"Ask Aberhart," suggested the heckler.

"Mr. Aberhart is a friend of mine," the Prime Minister replied. "He is a great teacher but he has not yet proved himself a great statesman."

Questioned when he referred to labor legislation involving a minimum wage law, Mr. Bennett declared that the unemployment relief camps provided food, clothing and shelter for single unemployed men.

"They were given sustenance and light work was provided to occupy them," he said, "and in addition they were given 20 cents a day spending money, and that is more than most of them were entitled to."

SECTION II

Schism and the Backbenchers' Revolt, 1935-1937

Aberhart at the First Anniversary Picnic on St. George's
Island, September, 1936.

Glenbow—Alberta Institute

1 PREMIER PROMISES DIVIDENDS

Edmonton Bulletin
December 23, 1935

Social Credit dividends inside 14 months were promised by Premier William Aberhart in an address here on Sunday, when he said that Major C.H. Douglas would "lay the foundations" for Social Credit during the next six months, "leaving me eight more months to fulfil my pledges."

But in the meantime he had a sharp reprimand for those Social Crediters who were growing impatient over the non-arrival of their Social Dividend cheques.

"You people who are impatient, you must quit this confounded grumbling; you who are whining like undeveloped, crying children," he said. "When a house is on fire the fire is put out first and the building of a fireproof building considered afterwards."

At the same time the premier pleaded for a chance to try out his plans.

"You all know me," he said. "Give me a chance. If I find out I can't do it, I'll throw up my hands and quit. In six months you will have recall legislation. You can banish me to the tall timbers. It is only six months since I got in and you are impatient."

"You can give me two years, or put me out."

When debt refunding was discussed at the dominion-provincial conference at Ottawa, the Alberta delegation was the only one with a definite and detailed proposal Premier Aberhart asserted.

"There can be no opposition to our plan," Mr. Aberhart told an audience of 1,300 persons who attended to hear the premier on his first visit to the institute since he returned from Ottawa. "The wages of labor have been reduced. Why shouldn't the wages of money be reduced?"

Mr. Aberhart congratulated Premier King on the way the conference was organized. "I am very pleased with the result both actual and potential," he said. "I would have liked to have more money for relief, but the dominion treasury is in a bad condition."

After extending the season's greetings to his listeners and the people of Alberta, Premier Aberhart stated Christmas greetings have a "hollow, mocking sound" under present conditions.

The premier said he noticed newspapers reported he was quiet and watchful at the Ottawa conferences. "When the opportunity presented itself, I spoke," he added. "We were out of the general political picture, were we not?"

---

2 ABERHART AND THE BUDGET

Albertan Social Credit Supplement
February 22, 1936

With the first major debate out of the way—the debate on the Speech from the Throne—the legislature is looking forward with exceptional interest to next week, probably Thursday, when the first budget of the first Social Credit government will be brought down.

Premier William Aberhart, interviewed on the subject, declared he hoped and expected that Hon. Charles Cockroff, Provincial Treasurer, would be in a position to bring down the budget on that date.

It will be an economy budget, with the government straining every effort to make it balance.

Since taking office on Sept. 3 Premier Aberhart has steadfastly pointed his course in one direction, namely, to balance the budget.

Even in the face of insistent demands for immediate action in paying the basic dividend, the premier has refused to be shaken from his resolve to set his financial house in order before embarking on the new venture.

"My first task is to balance the budget," he has said on previous occasions.

Thus, while no official pronouncement has been made, it goes without saying that the budget will aim primarily at economy with a view to balancing, as only with a balanced budget will credit be restored and the province proceed to new resolves.

Naturally, neither Premier Aberhart, nor Mr. Coockett [*sic*] will discuss the budget, as they wish to disclose it first to the legislature.

However, it has been learned on the most reliable authority that if the proposed provincial refunding scheme is consummated, then the provincial budget will be balanced. This appears a certainty.

3 DOUGLAS RESIGNS

Edmonton Journal
March 2, 1936

Major C.H. Douglas, British economist and originator of Social Credit, has resigned as chief reconstruction adviser to the Alberta government.

Immediate upshot of the resignation was "indefinite" post-ponement of government introduction of Social Credit enabling legislation, which has been planned for the house session Tuesday. A caucus of government supporters was called at which plans for the next move will be discussed.

Premier Aberhart declared at press time that the development would not affect his aim for an Alberta Social Credit plan.

Break between the world's first Social Credit administration and the economist followed a long and confusing series of communications between the Briton and Premier Aberhart. The resignation, first announced Tuesday by Major Douglas to the Journal's London correspondent, was confirmed immediately by the premier.

Dissatisfaction over the government accepting the reconstruction advice of R.J. Magor, economist, to which the Briton refers sarcastically in a statement issued in London, is believed to have led to the resignation.

In his announcement of his plan to terminate his contract with Alberta government, Major Douglas declares that it is useless for him to come to Alberta under prevailing conditions, says that no steps toward Social Credit have been taken here and claims that even though the province is "insolvent" Social Credit would be possible.

"I have nothing further to say until the cabinet has considered Major Douglas' letter Tuesday night. In the meantime we are not communicating with Major Douglas," stated Premier Aberhart, in revealing Tuesday that he had received the resignation Monday.

In London Major Douglas claimed he had made suggestions to the government which had not been followed. What these suggestions were was not explained.

4 ALL STRICTLY ORTHODOX

Edmonton Bulletin
March 3, 1936

There is no need to ask which of the Government's advisors drew up the plans and made out the specifications for the budget that was presented in the legislature yesterday by the Provincial Treasurer. Internal evidence identifies the author, by a process of elimination, as well as by direct implication. There is nothing in it looking to an increase of purchasing power in the hands of the public, by payment of dividends or other means. Major Douglas obviously had nothing to do with it.

The proclaimed purpose is directly opposite. It aims to take away from the public a part of the buying power they now have, and to export an undiminished amount of that buying power out of the province. Which is to say, it is a strictly "sound finance" budget, conforming in scope and detail with the tenets and traditions of orthodox economy.

It is precisely the kind of budget one would expect at the hands of the Executive Council of the Sound Finance organization of Montreal, and should bring applause from that quarter. If, as suggested, the "financial cannons" are to do any "roaring" about it, they will have to let off a salvo in celebration of another victory over the taxpayers, and that under circumstances where something different might have been looked for. "Make them pay and pay now" is the spirit and essence of it.

There is to be a 20 per cent increase in taxation. That is what the budget comes to; with a rather regretful remark added that it will really be necessary to ask the bond-holders to concede some reduction in the bond-interest rates out of the goodness of their hearts—sometime. Nothing about telling them they will have to cut the rate, and do it now. It is the taxpayer who is being "told."

There are two new taxes: a Social Service tax, and a Sales tax.

The Social Service tax will replace the Supplementary Revenue tax. The rates under the present tax are 2 mills. They will be 3 mills under the new tax. The property owner will contribute 50 per cent more than at present under the provincial tax on property.

As an off-set, the municipalities will be re-lieved of half what they now have to contribute to the mothers' pensions fund, and may, or may not, pass this saving back to their taxpayers.

Also, patients will hereafter be treated without fees at provincial tuberculosis hospitals, a concession to humanity that is long overdue, whatever it may do to taxbills.

After meeting these charges, the Government does not expect to have any of the Service tax money left.

The big feature of the budget is the new Sales tax, of 2 per cent, to be paid by the consumer, on commodities of all kinds. This is expected to collect $2,000,000 a year extra from the consuming public. Allowing ten per cent for expenses of collection, the net revenue is placed at $1,800,000.

The Sales tax is "earmarked" to meet the cost of unemployment relief. Unemployment is accepted now as a continuing evil. The cost is not to be capitalized in future, as in the past. Instead, the taxpayer will be made to "pay as they go," supplying the relief money as they buy goods at the stores through the Sales tax.

The idea is thus definitely abandoned that conditions will again come about in which every able-bodied resident of the province will be able to maintain himself. Provision is made to maintain as large a proportion as at present, rather larger in fact, by direct taxation applied immediately to those who have incomes and spend them.

What the Sales tax means is that a man who has an income of $1,000 a year, all of which goes to the support of his family, will have to pay $20 through the Sales tax, and his family get along on that much less.

---

5 NEW S.C. JARGON BEING DEVELOPED

Calgary Herald
March 10, 1936

Dealing with what he described as newpaper criticism of the Social Credit enabling bill introduced last week on the ground that it outlined no definite plan, the provincial secretary asked in his Sunday broadcast: "Don't you think it would be foolish for the government to make all the details of its procedure public so that our enemies would have further means of attacking us?"

Mr. Manning forgets that the present Alberta government is a government for the entire province and of all the people and not of a certain portion. Normal governments need no urging to present their more important policies to the people and to invite criticism of any weaknesses that may be discerned. They do not play hide-and-seek with their electorate, but lay their cards on the table—if they have any. It is just as much a right of the critics of Social Credit to be informed of the government's plans as it is of their followers, but in this case both groups are being kept in the dark. Moreover, there must be a considerable lack of confidence on the government's part in its own proposals when it is so anxious to keep them secret.

It is capable of proof that the so-called "enemies" of the Social Credit government have just as large a stake and as keen an interest in this province as have its supporters. Most of the former can lay claim to having contributed as much, if not more, to the development of Alberta as Mr. Manning, a comparatively recent addition to the population of the province. What right has he to describe men and women who for many years have played a constructive part in furthering its progress as "enemies"?

The use of this offensive word in this connection is a further evidence of the misuse of words which has developed since the advent of a politico-religious broadcasting on Sundays. The Liberals have just as much right to call Conservatives enemies, and vice versa, and followers of the C.C.F. might quite as correctly put Liberals, Conservatives and Social Crediters in that class. However, it is not a desirable practice to describe all who disagree with one's political beliefs as enemies. Normal folk can disagree in politics and still be reasonable.

A similar misuse of the King's English occurred in the Sunday broadcast of the premier in Edmonton. He declared that some people did not hear his addresses because of "biased indifference." Apart from the implied inference that everyone should listen to what he has to say, even public school students know that indifference cannot be "biased." It connotes a lack of interest in either side of a subject. Bias indicates an active interest in one side only.

---

6   HOPE IN ALBERTA'S EFFORT

Ottawa Citizen
April 10, 1936

There are scribes and pharisees aplenty to pour venom on a courageous leader, but critics of Premier Aberhart are far from reflecting the general feeling of the Canadian people toward Alberta's effort to deal with an impossible debt situation. Hon. H.H. Stevens came nearer expressing the Canadian view in the House of Commons the other day, when he said:

> Alberta's government has been treated with a good deal of scorn throughout the country, but it may well be that Mr. Aberhart in his attempt to attack the debt problem—whether he is right or wrong, whether his action is good or bad—will have shown about the only practical effort to solve these problems.

On the Liberal side, G.G. McGeer, M.P., also manifested the desire of people to be fair. He said:

> Now it must come with some measure of disturbance to the government to know that Alberta has defaulted on the payment of a loan which fell due, not because that provincial government was negligent in the imposition of taxes, nor because it was negligent in the use of the revenues that were available to that province. Alberta has no desire, on the part of either its government or its people, to repudiate its debts; on the contrary, it has shown that it is quite willing to have the ideas of the existing government with respect to Social Credit stand aside until that government, with the assistance of competent, orthodox financial and economic authority, exhausts every possible channel through which the means of meeting its obligations and balancing its budgets can be sustained.

The Dominion minister of finance, Hon. Charles Dunning, has acknowledged the sincerity of Premier Aberhart. Many other people have been similarly impressed. They are learning, too, that he is a political leader of strong, determined character: he is going quietly and steadily on, in accordance with the mandate given to him by an overwhelming majority in the last provincial election.

One cheap form of criticism is to make it appear that Mr. Aberhart is a religious fanatic. It might be sufficient to reply that the so-called practical minds of the world have so little to offer in the nature of leadership, the nations have been so badly misled by doctrines of scarcity and policies of rationalization, the bewildered sheep could do worse than turn to an old-fashioned religious faith. But the Social Credit premier of Alberta is no fanatical shepherd of sheep. He took up the task of political leadership, from being headmaster of Calgary High School, in response to the urgent demand of sober and intelligent people.

There are such people everywhere in Canada hoping that Premier Aberhart will press on, nor does he need to be reminded of the promise in Isaiah 30 when the forward path is followed. "This is the way, walk ye in it" ...has a daily meaning for the prime minister of Alberta.

---

7   A TECHNICAL DEFAULT

Calgary Herald
April 21, 1936

Technical default financially was comparable to the technical knock-out of prize ring—it was something that was done to save the victim further useless punishment.

Such was the simile of the ring used by Premier Aberhart of Alberta today in a luncheon address before the Vancouver Canadian Club during which he explained the course of his government in defaulting debt payments due April 1.

Addressing one of the largest audiences ever gathered at a Canadian Club luncheon meeting here, the rotund, placid Social Credit leader made a simple statement of facts about finances of his province. It was at once an explanation and a defence.

The Alberta premier said he had no advice to give British Columbia but he made the emphatic prediction that the financial crisis now facing Alberta was imminent for every province of the Dominion—perhaps the Dominion itself. He warned that governments cannot borrow themselves out of debt. He said that he did not believe in repudiation. He said that his government had "caught the situation in time" and held out hope of recovery.

He staunchly held against the proposed federal loan council as a demand for the province's birthright.

If, he said, there was one man who should understand a technical default it was he, as premier of Alberta. He emphasized the fact that it was "technical" and not a deliberate intention.

"Most men know what a technical knock-out means. It is not a real knock-out. The man does not go down for the count of ten. A technical knock-out is this: the referee concludes that the opponent is in a helpless condition, and to save further cruelty and suffering he calls it a knock-out even though it is not actually one."

"Now a technical default is similar to these. It is not wilful or intentional. The debtor is quite willing to meet his debt if he could do so. The fact is that the debtor is in such a helpless state that to save further suffering the default is called, even though in reality it is not one."

Premier Aberhart summarized his conclusions under three main headings:

"1. No individual corporation of state can hope to borrow itself out of debt. A persistence in this pernicious habit will mean the ultimate destruction of our credit. Your government must face this fact in the immediate future."

"2. We cannot go ahead paying the heavy toll placed upon us by the money barons without ultimately losing all we have. Interest rates must come down on a par with the wages of services and the price of goods. I understand that you are undertaking to build a bridge across the Fraser River at an expense of from two to three million dollars. My proposal to establish a provincial bank for the purpose of providing cheap money for enterprises such as this seems to have met with some disrespect in your province. May I remind you that before you get your bridge

paid for it will cost you from nine to twelve million dollars. State enterprises must be financed by an issue of her own medium of purchasing power."

"We can never raise the standard of living of all our people until we establish a new and scientific method of distributing purchasing power. It is to this task that we are fast hastening in the province of Alberta. The difficulties connected with our technical default have somewhat delayed our progress, but we shall soon be demonstrating by action what we have so often elucidated in talk. I realize that many are saying it cannot be done. Surely we should be given an opportunity to try, especially since no one else has a better proposition to make."

Mr. Aberhart traced the financial troubles which had faced his new government in Alberta, beginning with a maturity which fell due in January. His government had offered to co-operate in every way but they could not agree to the proposed loan council. To meet the January crisis they had paid over all the money they could find and Ottawa covered the balance.

"Since that time Saskatchewan and British Columbia both have had maturities fall due. I have inquired how it was that these provinces had such little trouble compared with Alberta and I was told that there was a secret hidden in that."

"A secret. Well, these secrets are sometimes costly. All I can say is that we have had no one to enter into any secret understanding with us. All our negotiations and proposals have been brought into the limelight of public opinion and criticism."

---

8   PREMIER'S REASSURING DENIAL

Edmonton Journal
January 2, 1937

It is decidedly reassuring to learn from Mr. Aberhart that there is no intention of introducing drastic legislation at the coming session. He says that he has no knowledge of any measures of this kind. Of course he can be speaking only for himself and for the government. The private members who told the divisional conference on Tuesday of the radical proposals that were contemplated are quite free to submit them to the party caucus the week after next. If they are approved there, the house may be asked to deal with them even if they are not endorsed by the government. But the statement from the premier must appreciably lessen the concern that was caused by the proceedings at the conference.

At the same time Hon. Dr. Cross, the chairman of the committee which has been preparing a Social Credit plan, declared that one of its members, Mr. Ansley, "spoke without the authority of the committee or the government" at Tuesday's divisional gathering. "We must knock our opponents off their pedestals," delegates were told by Mr. Ansley, who held that drastic legislation was accordingly necessary. He intimated that he had been in close contact with some cabinet ministers as to what was proposed. This and the fact that he is associated with three ministers on the planning committee naturally led to the conclusion that the radical policies which he said would be announced before long had that body's approval.

The view expressed by The Journal on Thursday, that the speeches delivered at the divisional conference made a showdown between the two Social Credit wings imminent, must be strengthened by the premier's denial of knowledge of legislation such as was foreshadowed at that gathering. That it could not be to Mr. Aberhart's liking is clear from statements made by him prior to and since his assumption of office. A few days after he became premier he said:

> We have assured the citizens time and again that upon no conditions will there be confiscation or repudiation of any kind which will destroy the credit of this splendid province.

That is the position he has taken repeatedly in the interval and a few weeks ago when the flight of cash and securities from the province had attained large proportions, this statement from him appeared in the Social Credit newspaper:

> Bonds and securities cannot be confiscated or attached by the government without confiscating the property they represent and the Social Credit

government has never considered and has no idea of ever confiscating property.

While policies have been adopted which are not in keeping with the first of these declarations, there is reason to believe that Mr. Aberhart himself has all along been anxious and still is, to adhere to it strictly. Now that departures from it on a much more extended scale are being proposed and that will, if carried through, completely destroy the credit of this "splendid province," it is clearly up to him and to all his political associates who realize the dangers that such a course involves to make a determined stand against the "drastic" measures of which warning has been given. Confidence that they will do so has been much increased by the statement from the premier that appeared in The Journal on Thursday.

---

9 SOCIAL CREDIT COULD WORK SUCCESSFULLY

Calgary Herald
January 2, 1937

John Hargrave, technical adviser to the government committee established to formulate a social credit plan for Alberta, sees no real obstacles to the new financial order in the province.

"Would it be possible for social credit to operate successfully in this province?" he was asked today.

"Yes, certainly. I have no doubt whatever that it could be operated successfully in Alberta," the leader of the United Kingdom Social Credit Party replied.

Asked for his reasons, Hargrave continued: "Alberta is a vastly rich province, rich in natural wealth beyond dreams. You have a gigantic export surplus of wealth in the form of wheat and meat which you could always exchange for imported goods paid for in Canadian money."

"But at present Alberta is like a kitten that has been pushed into a water-hole with a brick tied round its neck—and that brick is the burden of the fictitious bank-debt."

"You should cut away that burden and make your home-market effective by the issue of Alberta debt-free money. There is no real difficulty in doing this. All it requires is a technical knowledge, plus courage," said Mr. Hargrave.

Hargrave came to Alberta a month ago to study conditions here and watch the development of a social credit financial system. When Premier Aberhart named a committee to formulate a social credit plan, Hargrave consented to be technical adviser without pay.

Hargrave is in the advertising business in London. He was a commercial artist and cartoonist in his younger days, and has written two or three novels. During the war he served on the Gallipoli front and in Egypt.

---

10 S.C. LEAGUE TO DISCUSS RESOLUTIONS

Calgary Herald
January 15, 1937

Suggested amendments to the constitution of the Alberta Social Credit League were discussed at the Thursday morning session of the provincial Social Credit convention.

The delegates expressed the view that they would accomplish much more useful work by discussing improvements in their parent organization by way of constitutional amendments than by discussing resolutions which would have no bearing upon current problems.

It was said the delegates had in mind the advice given them by Premier Aberhart on Wednesday. At that time the premier warned them against wasting their time on party politics and in the discussion of resolutions that had nothing to do with Social Credit or the problems facing the government.

While there was considerable discussion among the delegates on the code situation, prior to the convention being called to order, the premier's statement that the government had decided not to enforce the codes was not officially discussed.

It was planned, however, to give over the majority of the afternoon to discussion of resolutions, with the possibility that election of officers would be held over for the night session, if found necessary.

There was no evening session on Thursday. Delegates accepted the invitation to hear a lecture on Social Credit by John Hargrave, No. 1 technical adviser to the government.

---

11 SOCIAL CREDIT?

Calgary Herald
January 15, 1937

Has Alberta a Social Credit government? Has it a Social Credit plan? Has it even a Social Credit policy?

Anyone who has given even a little study to the theories originated by Major C.H. Douglas must have asked himself these questions over and over again during the past sixteen months. For behind the blaring assurances of Premier Aberhart, behind all that strange ballyhoo of mixed abuse and pleading with which it has filled the ether, the Aberhart government has quite evidently been dodging and doubling all the time like a hard-pressed jack-rabbit. It has had no plan, no clear-cut policy, not even any intelligent grasp of what the Social Credit theory meant.

First it increased taxes. Then it imposed codes. Then it sought loans. Then it defaulted on its debts. Then it went wildly enthusiastic over scrip—and dropped it within three months. Next came all the lively make-believe of covenants and pretended quick action.

And now we have the simple, blunt assurance of the government's own chief adviser on Social Credit that all this was like the groping of a blind man on a black night. That neither codes nor covenants nor scrip have anything to do with Social Credit.

John Hargrave, for years a leader of the social credit movement in England, came to Edmonton early in December to see for himself what was going on there. At once his advice was sought by Premier Aberhart in the preparation of a social credit plan for Alberta.

Premier Aberhart was supposed to have had a plan three months ago, but seemingly it had got lost.

Mr. Hargrave during December sat with a committee of the cabinet to discuss a plan for social credit. His views were accepted by that committee and at the invitation of the Premier himself he appeared before this week's caucus of Social Credit members to explain the committee's report. No one in Edmonton can deny that he has been recognized by the government itself as an expert and an authority.

But in a carefully prepared interview, Mr. Hargrave informed us yesterday that he has found no Social Credit in Alberta, that the chief need he sees here is "that the government should be publicly committed to the basic principles of Social Credit," that the Aberhart government has not yet been committed to those principles, and that in his opinion its behavior during the past sixteen months has been like that of a man "stumbling along on a pitch black night."

In the light of these opinions from the government's own adviser, many people will wonder afresh just what connection there is between Aberhartism and Social Credit.

12 FRANKNESS FROM PREMIER

Calgary Herald
January 15, 1937

Premier Aberhart was in a candid mood when he addressed the opening session of the first province-wide convention of the Social Credit League in Edmonton yesterday.

He confessed that when he first began the spreading of the gospel of Social Credit as a cure-all for economic ills through the medium of his pulpit in the Prophetic Bible Institute he did not expect that his movement would sweep into power in the 1935 election. The most he hoped for was that the "ranks of the other parties would be thinned out."

Mr. Aberhart thus at long last has confirmed an impression quite generally entertained by many of his critics at the time. Neither they nor the present Premier thought for a moment that his pulpit crusade would sweep the province. They regarded it as a new theme—minor prophecy being worn somewhat thin—by which interest in and support of the Institute's activities would be maintained and even stimulated to new growth.

Mr. Aberhart's lack of confidence in the success of the Social Credit movement at the polls on August 22, 1935, was fully indicated by his refusal to stand as a candidate. In the event of failure to capture the majority of seats in the Legislature, the Social Credit leader was in a position to continue as principal of the Crescent Heights High School at a comfortable salary.

But once the election was over with its Social Credit sweep, it required no urging to induce him to step into the Premiership. Even when assured of several years in office with all its rich emoluments, the new Premier applied for and was granted an indefinite leave of absence from teaching duties, thus keeping the door open for his return and preserving his seniority rights in the teaching service.

He further told his followers in Edmonton: "I have no desire to be in politics, but only to put in Social Credit." If and when that objective is realized, he proposes to get out of office and live somewhere "in an atmosphere of peace and happiness." This permits one to suspect that he has not had much of either in the past sixteen months, and the reason is not far to seek. He made too many and too extravagant pre-election promises which he has not fulfilled. He has been given a taste of official responsibility which is a far different thing than pre-election irresponsible criticism from the Bible Institute.

It is quite conceivable that Premier Aberhart has often longed in months past for the peace and quiet of his old sanctum in the Crescent Heights High School, or for peaceful haven in Vancouver where members of his family live, where he would be free from importunate office seekers, newspaper critics and disillusioned followers.

13 ABERHART SAYS INTEREST CUT FIGHT TO PROCEED

Albertan
January 25, 1937

Launching out in a forceful offensive against the money monopolists who by means of leaflet propaganda, he said, are attempting to undermine public confidence in the government, Premier William Aberhart, in addressing the Edmonton Prophetic Bible Conference at the Strand Theatre here Sunday night, declared that even though the powerful money monopolists might win their case to have the Debt Reduction and Settlement Act declared ultra vires, the government's fight for lower interest rates would not stop.

The debt consolidation act was another statute that could be used. The premier, who was greeted by a capacity audience, was in his top oratorical form.

Fighting a battle in which he has been in the forefront, namely, for lower interest rates, the premier lashed out freely at the monied interests.

He declared interest and debt charges must come down if the province and the Dominion as a whole were to survive.

"As a matter of fact, some of the financial magnates admit to their friends frankly that if we go forward carefully and confidently the money barons cannot stop us. They openly assert that the only way they will defeat us is to break the confidence of the people and make them afraid to use their own credit. They add that the people have become so used to bank money and cheques and banks that when we shout loud enough the people will be stampeded and we shall drive them back into our corral. My only reply is that our people are not such big fools. They are beginning to know your tricks."

Taking up the propaganda of the financial interests, the premier said:

Step by step you people of Alberta are nearing the critical moment, the crossing of the Jordan. Are you afraid of the giants ahead? You need not be, for our God can help us. But will you be stampeded, frightened, scattered far and wide by the agitators and the propagandists. Already the old political parties are getting their banners out and shouting. They say it will not be long now before they will befoggle the people and bemuddle the issues so that the present government will be discredited and the old political machine will once more function. They are scambling for your ear and your confidence.

"All I can say is 'if you want the old machine again, let us know, so we can get out of the way. If you are satisfied with what they have in the neighboring provinces, it is all right with us. We have been trying to get you more than that.

14 HARGRAVE LEAVES EDMONTON: ABERHART'S RESPONSE

Calgary Herald
January 26, 1937

John Hargrave, technical adviser to the social credit planning committee of the Aberhart government, suddenly left Edmonton today because "I regretfully find myself unable to co-operate further with Mr. Aberhart and his cabinet."

In a statement to the press, Hargrave said: "Having done my utmost to help, I am leaving Alberta because I find it impossible to co-operate with a government which I consider a mere vacillating machine which operates in starts, stops and reversals."

The Hargrave statement, delivered to the press after he left his hotel and apparently caught a train for the east, said "I still feel the first social credit government in the world is not yet publicly committed to the principles of social credit. I still feel that it lacks technical knowledge and that, as a consequence, it has, over the past 16 months, groped its way, like a man stumbling along on a pitchblack night. There were, I felt, and as I stated in the first interview, indications that it was groping its way 'in the right general direction,' but, as a result of the meeting held on January 22, I should now hesitate to say even that."

Hargrave is the leader of the Social Credit party of the United Kingdom and came to Edmonton to "see for myself how the first social credit government in the world was attempting to implement the principles of social credit."

He became technical adviser to the cabinet committee which Premier Aberhart established to draft a social credit plan for the province. The plan was completed on January 8, and presented to the caucus of Social Credit members which opened on January 11. "From that date to this," Hargrave's statement said, "I have had no official information regarding the acceptance or rejection of the report or any possible legislation implementing it. I have been kept in official darkness."

Calgary Herald
January 26, 1937

Premier William Aberhart struck back last night at John Hargrave, technical adviser to the government's social credit planning committee who suddenly left Edmonton yesterday "because I regretfully find myself unable to co-operate further with Mr. Aberhart and his cabinet."

The Alberta premier, leader of the first Social Credit government in the world, declared his faith in social credit remained unshaken and "I fear this is but another attempt by some unknown person or persons, through the instrumentality of some undisclosed medium, to make our task all the more difficult."

In a statement to the press last night Premier Aberhart said: "I am sorry to say we are forced to conclude that Mr. Hargrave is an irresponsible person who has had some sinecure motive in coming to our province."

Hargrave, leader of the Social Credit Party of the United Kingdom, left Edmonton yesterday claiming "what little confidence I had left in the competence, determination and reliability of the Aberhart government" had been lost.

At first, Premier Aberhart declined comment on the Hargrave statement but last night he issued the following:

"I have read the statement published by John Hargrave immediately after his sudden departure from Edmonton. I am astounded at its contents."

"On January 22, at the meeting referred to by him, the members of the committee of the cabinet working on the introduction of social credit, affirmed again most definitely their allegiance to the great principles of social credit."

"They called Mr. Hargrave's attention to the fact that his declaration of the principles was not new to our people and he agreed to make an explanation in writing of his recent utterances to the newspapers."

"These explanations were willingly promised by him to be ready for our next meeting on Monday, January 25."

"I was greatly surprised, therefore, when the newspaper advised me of his statement received by them after his departure."

"I fear this is but another attempt by some unknown person or persons, through the instrumentality of some undisclosed medium, to make our task all the more difficult."

"I am sorry to say we are forced to conclude that Mr. Hargrave is an irresponsible person who has had some sinecure motive in coming to our province."

"I am glad, however, that we have not become too greatly involved in our relationship with him."

"It should at once appear strange to the readers of his statement that a comparative stranger could be able to declare that the members of the government lacked competence, determination and reliability."

"The people of this province who knew the members of this government for years and who elected them on the very grounds that this faithless man has maligned them, should resent very much an attack of this kind coming from this ambitious egotist, even though he be a self-styled advocate of Douglas social credit."

"I am confident that as premier, I can leave the judgment of this case fully in the hands of all the supporters of the government, knowing that they realize that we are citizens of this province, desirous of doing the very best we can for the improvement of conditions and also that it is our intention to continue our citizenship in the province for many years to come."

"We haven't lost our firm belief in social credit principles."

15 WHY NOT GENERAL ELECTION?

Calgary Herald
March 2, 1937

Premier Aberhart's proposal that only members of the Alberta Social Credit League should be consulted on whether or not the government should carry on savors of a similar early referendum conducted by Herr Hitler who rode to a dictatorship on the shoulders of a small minority of the German people.

The paid-up membership of the Social Credit League is approximately 35,000 and it may be allowed that there are several more thousands of government followers who may not be in good financial standing.

But there were 301,852 votes cast in the last provincial election and of this number 163,800 were in favor of Social Credit. Why confine the referendum on the government's record to the Social Credit League members or even to social crediters as a whole? Government of this province is a concern of all its people.

Why not call a general election to ascertain if the Aberhart party's "stop, start and reverse" record is approved by the majority of the electors?

16 NO DIVIDENDS AND NONE IN PROSPECT

Edmonton Journal
March 2, 1937

There is much that must be challenged strongly in the statement that Mr. Aberhart made on Sunday. It cannot satisfy those who have given him their support, if they examine it with an open mind and in the light of the undertakings on the strength of which he was placed in control of the affairs of the province.

I believe, declared the premier, that a promise is a contract that should be fulfilled, if at all possible, and it is my intention to fulfill my promise today. I promised our supporters faithfully that in eighteen months I would try to establish Social Credit in Alberta and, if for some reason, I was unable to do so I would tell them frankly and leave the matter in their hands, whether I should continue my efforts further or resign.

But it was certainly not because of any promise "to try to establish Social Credit" in eighteen months that the electors gave Mr. Aberhart a sweeping majority in the legislature. There was the most definite promise that dividends (a word that he did not use on Sunday) would be paid within that period, which expires today.

Long after he had assumed office he was still leading people to believe that the dividends would be forthcoming on their due date or before. On July 15 last he reiterated that they would be paid by the end of the allotted year and a half and on September 22 told a Vancouver audience that the distribution would take place within the next two months.

This being so, the public was entitled to expect something more from the premier, when the eighteen months was almost up, than the acknowledgement that his hopes have not been realized and the announcement that it will be left to S.C. constituency associations to say "what they desire us to do." Even they were not asked for a prompt answer. The suggestion was that they meet after the legislation of the present session is made known and that they take no vote until the first of June.

It is definitely up to our supporters, Mr. Aberhart concluded, if they wish to give us a further mandate, or direction along another line. In the meanwhile we shall carry on.

But the mandate that the government received a year and a half ago was from the electorate as a whole. It is answerable to all the citizens for its failure to carry out its pledge. Any "further mandate" must come from them and not from the Social Credit organizations, to which many who voted for Social Credit candidates or who "co-operated" with the government by registering last summer do not belong.

The putting up to these bodies of the question of whether or not the government, having failed to pay dividends, is to continue in office is an absurd procedure the results of which can mean nothing.

It is quite plain that Mr. Aberhart when elected had no Social Credit plan that was within the powers of the province and that he has not had one at any time since then. If on Sunday he had acknowledged this frankly and stated that while he had given his preelection promises in good faith, he now found it impossible to carry them out, he would have stood much higher in the estimation of the people of Alberta than he does talking as he did then.

Once again the premier spoke of the difficulties that had been experienced through "opponents and blocking tactics." But, with the enormous majority at his command in the legislature, the government had not the slightest reason to worry about anything that its political adversaries did.

The fact is, of course, as ought to be apparent to everyone, that what is responsible for its failure is that it undertook to do something that was quite impossible under the province's constitutional and other limitations. These limitations constitute the only effective opposition to which the government has been subjected. But they have proven quite sufficient, as it was predicted during the election campaign they would, to bring about the abject failure of the program on which it came into power.

---

17 S.C. MEMBER CRITICIZES GOVERNMENT

Calgary Herald
March 5, 1937

The provincial government will retain the services of an administrative Social Credit expert in the near future.

This announcement was made in government circles this morning following a five-hour caucus of government members on Thursday night.

It was also stated that the government's two most important pieces of legislation, the bill to provide for the setting up of an import and export bureau and a bill to provide for the establishment of Alberta "credit", would most likely be introduced in the legislature this afternoon.

Adjournment of the House until 3 o'clock on Tuesday afternoon is then expected to be announced by Premier Aberhart, although there may be a last minute change in this plan.

The government's announcement that retention of a Social Credit "administrative" expert had been approved by the private members is said to indicate that some sort of a social credit plan is to be laid before the House shortly.

The duties of this expert would not be that of technical adviser. Instead, his job would be to administer the Alberta social credit plan if and when it is finally placed on the statutes.

It is in line with the advice given the government by John Hargrave, leader of the "Green Shirts" movement of London, England, during the short period on which he acted as No. 1 technical adviser to the government without pay.

If "fireworks" developed during the five-hour session of the caucus, following warm criticism of the government, voiced by A.L. Blue (SC) Ribstone, as had been anticipated, there is still no record of it.

The government members emerged from the caucus chamber about 1 o'clock on Friday morning after being in session since 8:15 o'clock.

Mr. Blue was among them. He told newspapermen that he had nothing to say, but his presence during the long session indicated that if he had been disciplined by the party for his utterances in the House on Thursday afternoon, his "sentence" did not include suspension from the party caucus.

During the throne speech debate on Thursday afternoon, Mr. Blue said that he was opposed to the province being represented at the Coronation, he was opposed to a caucus form of government, too much talk and not enough action in face of the difficulties confronting the people of the province.

The government was taken by surprise. A meeting of the cabinet was hastily called and Mr. Blue was informed by J.H. Unwin, government whip, that he would be expected to be at the council chamber at 8 p.m. A caucus of government members was also called.

When the cabinet convened at 8 o'clock, Mr. Blue was in the buildings, but was not called. When the caucus opened a short time later, Mr. Blue entered with other members.

The cabinet's sudden decision to "get on the job" is believed to have been inspired by the publication of reports that private members have been holding caucuses of their own, and the fact that one of the Crown members publicly criticized the government on the floor of the House during the afternoon.

At the caucus on Thursday evening, the members were given a brief outline of the proposed legislation and were advised that the session would swing into more serious business after the throne speech debate is concluded.

Aberhart in his office.

From Stewart Cameron, No Matter How Thin You Slice It.
By permission of Mrs. Thelma Cameron.

Though the stage was now set for an "advance" toward realization of "Social Credit," and insurgent attacks were daily becoming more feeble, there was little indication that the Premier either had a plan or hoped to evolve one. The cartoonist thought he discerned the government's line of march.   (April 9, 1937.)

"DOUBLE, DOUBLE, TOIL AND TROUBLE; FIRE BURN AND CAULDRON BUBBLE."

From Stewart Cameron, No Matter How Thin You Slice It.
By permission of Mrs. Thelma Cameron.

At the end of the first two years of the "Social Credit" Government's regime, there was still no "Social Credit" in sight. Dividends had not been paid and unemployment was increasing steadily. Conditions throughout the province were very unsettled. Heartily dissatisfied with Premier Aberhart's record, his constituents in the High River-Okotoks district instituted recall proceedings against him. Simultaneously a meeting at Milk River demanded a provincial election. Mr. Aberhart found himself much in the plight of Shakespeare's unhappy Macbeth who entered the witch's cave only to hear her fortell his ultimate doom. (October 9, 1937.)

18 TIME TO BE CAUTIOUS

Albertan
March 6, 1937

Newspapers opposed to the Alberta government have carried articles these last few days designed to promote revolution within the caucus and the party ranks.

The opposition would, of course, do everything possible to embarrass the Aberhart government, and if this could be accomplished by stirring up a few of the members within the group, then the people of Alberta may expect that to be the next line of attack.

It may be that there are members of the government group who would like more speed and compulsion along Social Credit lines than the cabinet is prepared to give. If that is true, these members would be wise to give long and careful consideration before demanding too much speed in a situation where speed might do tremendous harm.

The Government has taken the attitude that the introduction of economic changes in Alberta will be the gradual process in a friendly spirit of co-operation in which all the people of Alberta will participate.

The government, like all the governments in the history of civilization, has made mistakes. Humanity, in the high places and the humble, is prone to error and governments do not escape the fallibility of the human race. Perhaps the greatest mistake the present government of Alberta made was in trying to accomplish too much in too short a space of time and in committing itself to a time period in which to initiate Social Credit principles in Alberta's economic life.

It will be to the good of everyone if Alberta makes sound progress toward a new economic goal; progress in which every citizen takes part in a spirit of friendly co-operation and good will, even if that progress must be more gradual than desired by some blessed with the virtue of impatience untempered by caution and clear thinking.

If there are members within the caucus who would make the long, hard road of the present Government longer and harder by urging speed, regimentation and drastic legislation, they will be contributing only to the disintegration of their own movement; playing into the hands of the old-deal reactionaries who are encouraging them now.

19 FIREWORKS AHEAD

Calgary Herald
March 17, 1937

With echoes of Premier Aberhart's "no dividends" statement still being heard in the shape of "murmurings" from Social Credit supporters to their constituency representatives, government members of the House are growing more puzzled daily over the continued delay in introduction of the Alberta Social Credit Act bill.

While the legislature drives ahead to prorogation by Easter if possible, government members have not yet seen a draft of the bill under which the government hopes to provide Alberta citizens with a continual flow of credit.

Murmurs of discontent from a section of the government side of the House have swelled to such a pitch, that published reports of a serious split in government ranks no longer bring official denials. It is definitely established that there is an insurgent group within the ranks, and that it will be heard from publicly and very definitely in the near future.

A government member frankly stated today that much of the discontent has arisen because of the non-appearance of the Credit Act bill.

It was first stated, that the bill would be introduced in the House on or about February 30[*sic*]. Not only has it not been introduced, but it has not yet reached the caucus in draft form.

One section of the House consisting of about 20 members, not satisfied with the progress that the government has been making in implementing social credit legislation, have been holding their own private caucus uptown. These members are reported to favor direct action in forcing the government to bring in a plan without further delay.

These members are also objecting to the budget being brought in and passed before the House has had an opportunity of considering social credit legislation.

W.J. Lampley (SC), Peace River, stands ready to resign if the government does not take direct action shortly, it is said.

A.L. Blue (SC), Ribstone, attacked the government publicly in the House on Tuesday for bringing down the budget ahead of the social credit legislation, and for drafting a budget without considering the possible effect that the budget would have on expected social credit legislation. Other attacks upon the budget by government members before the debate ends would not come as a surprise to those who have been observing the situation closely.

There was some applause for Mr. Blue from the government side of the House on Tuesday when he criticized the government's policy.

In another section of the government side, his remarks were received in stony silence.

There was no applause from the treasury bench.

The delay in bringing in the third social credit bill is causing some uneasiness even among the most staunch supporters of the government.

There is a section that is intensely loyal to the premier and will support him no matter what happens. These members consist principally of the older members of the government side, and they are quite willing to sit back and wait until the government is ready to bring in its plan and to support it to the limit when it does come to the House.

A number of the younger members, however, are frankly impatient over the delay.

"This planning committee has been working on this bill for months and still we have not yet seen a draft copy," one member said.

"It is about time that something definite was placed before the House."

"It's about time we got under way with the scheme. We have waited long enough," another member said.

There are some private members who actually believed that the premier was bringing a social credit plan with him when named to office 18 months ago.

To them, disillusionment has come, and added to their worries is the fact they must soon face their constituents and place before them the government's record of the past year.

In the meantime, the numerous "huddles" continue. Members gather in two and threes up town to discuss the general situation and there are murmurs, promises of "fireworks" to come unless the government accelerates its pace in introduction of social credit legislation.

20 BOARD TO HAVE WIDE POWERS OF CONTROL

Edmonton Journal
March 17, 1937

Proposing to establish a board to control transportation, packing, storage and marketing of natural products and all other commodities in Alberta, a bill introduced in the legislature by Hon. Dr. W.W. Cross, minister of trade and industry, was handed down in printed form Wednesday.

Sweeping powers to control the sale of any commodity within the province are proposed in the new bill. It provides for the setting up of a provincial marketing board and provincial trading board.

The latter would have power to buy, sell and deal in, farm produce, livestock and all other commodities. The bill provides that the trading board shall consist of three members and would be allowed to operate on a margin of profit sufficient to meet operating expenses.

If the new bill is enacted it would repeal the Alberta Natural Products Marketing act, and the Control and Marketing of Wheat act.

The bill would allow the government to have complete control over all marketing. One provision would allow the government to prohibit any transportation, packing, storage or marketing of any commodity it saw fit.

The government would have to require any or all persons engaged in packing, transportation, storing or marketing of any commodity to register and obtain licenses from the marketing board. At the same time the board would have power to demand full information relating to the production, transporting, storing and marketing of all commodities and could inspect the books of all persons engaged therein.

The board would be empowered to fix the prices and grades of all commodities, and could fix different prices for different parts of the province. Any commodity kept, transported, packed, stored or marketed in violation of any order of the board could be seized and disposed of by the board.

21 ABERHART DEFENDS HIS POLICIES

Edmonton Bulletin
March 22, 1937

Declarations by P.J. Rowe, M.P. for Athabasca, that he was going to oust him as head of the provincial government and president of the provincial executive council, has not caused any alarm or misgiving, Premier William Aberhart informed his audience at the Edmonton Prophetic Bible Conference, at the Strand theatre on Sunday evening.

"I need not tell you," said the Premier, "that I read the newspaper item in which P.J. Rowe, the honorable member of Parliament for Athabasca, declared he was going to oust me from the premiership and either take the job himself or appoint another.

"It is refreshing to hear a man speak with such assurance and confidence and to feel his power so definitely. I would personally be much alarmed if I did not know two facts, first, I can only be ousted by the will of the people of this province, as when you say you want me out, then I must forthwith retire; second, when you give me the faintest hint that you want P.J. Rowe, the honorable member for Athabasca, or his appointee, I shall not even offer any objection. I am persuaded that this movement is not of man, but of God and therefore, I nor no other individual can be essential."

The Premier, in the course of his address, warmly defended the government's trades and occupation licensing bill, now before the legislature and also attacked the intrigue going on against the government.

Dealing with response to his pronouncement made in Calgary several weeks ago, regarding delay in paying the basic dividend, the Premier said that "I had thought by this time the letters from the groups and individuals regarding my query to them some four weeks ago would have dwindled down, but instead there are more than ever. I suppose at this time of the year the roads are none too good and many people are very busy, so it takes longer to get a voluntary response."

Dealing with the recent action of a Red Deer group, in demanding action in establishing social credit, the Premier said that "It is but fair to say just here that many of the groups in and around Red Deer feel deeply that one group should give the impression through the press that the whole constituency desires the resignation of the present cabinet. Numbers of individuals and groups around Red Deer have written in protesting the unfair publicity that they are getting. I regret this very much, but I presume that some of you will have to bear this just as we have to bear the many falsities and misrepresentations that are thrown at us from day to day and from near and far."

The Premier said "as we press on in our planning for the establishment of social credit, persistent rumors of intrigue and disloyalty are heard from time to time on every side. I have steadfastly tried to disbelieve it, although I know that it may be expected.

"You have but to glance over the pages of Canadian and British history to find that this has always been so. That's why we have the problems we have. Take any great reform that has ever been attempted or accomplished for the protection or the welfare of the common people generally. Study its history and you will find that sooner or later some one or more would give over or sell out or betray the cause and hinder or destroy the movement.

"Why even in fighting the Indians who were determined to scalp and massacre the men, women and children of a settlement, men have been known to forsake their ranks and join the foes, betraying to them all the information and plans of their fellows. Many a brave man has been made a martyr by the betrayal of his fellows. History tells us that this has continually been a characteristic of humanity. Some men cannot resist the opportunity to become great at the expense of their fellow men."

After dealing with Mr. Rowe's declaration to oust him, the Premier declared that "This is the first time I have ever heard that when we elected members to the Dominion parliament they were to interfere and direct the government of the province and do nothing in the federal department.

"I see where some of the papers are telling you that some of our members are going to resign because things are not moving fast enough. I wonder if that is a reason or an excuse, or if there is any truth in the declaration at all.

"We have done as much as could be done. Your government has worked faithfully and well. That is all that I can say. If any member desires to leave us in the midst of the fight of course it is his privilege, but what does he hope to accomplish thereby. Does he think an action will help or hinder.

"True, from the point of view of the movement, those who are willing to face the problem and press on, those who wish to forsake the cause would be well advised to do it at once. It seems to me that these newspaper stories cannot be true, for if they are, the people will at once be informed of the enormous problem that faces us.

"One writer this week who seemed to have more than ordinary discernment wrote, 'We are willing to give you time to get all your forces in line with the movement. We have no other man that we want to do it. So carry on. We are 100 per cent back of you.'

"Thank you, sir, and also your group. I can only reply that I came into this office for one purpose and one purpose only. I wanted to try to alter the present impossible financial system. I have found grave difficulty, bitter opposition and gross misrepresentation. But I feel that our efforts have not been complete as yet. It may be that new forms of attack and hindrance may be introduced and some of our forces may forsake, but as long as the majority say 'carry on' I'll face the foe. Probably, like Admiral Nelson, I shall put the telescope to my blind eye, as it were, and give no heed to those who would hinder or prevent success."

The Premier then read a list of 57 groups, varying from 35 to 80 members each, which had written him supporting his retention of office even though delay is occasioned in paying dividends. Later in his address he read a further list of 65 more groups, later another list of 15, and last a list of nine groups in this city, for a total of 136 from all parts of the province.

He also read extracts from letters, the whole trend of all quotations being to carry on and press ahead to the goal of delivery from economic bondage.

He also said that all dates for sponsoring the Conference broadcasts had been snapped up until June.

Turning his attention to the government proposal to license businesses, occupations and trades the Premier said that "We are hearing a great deal of bally-hoo—about liberty today. Liberty of conscience, liberty of occupation, liberty of the press and British liberty. I humbly ask what about liberty of the individual consumer?

"Some brag about liberty in a time of the greatest economic bondage in history. Why are we so easily beguiled by fine phrases?

"What liberty have many of you regarding occupation? What liberty have you to use the press? What do you mean by liberty anyway? The dictionary defines liberty as freedom from despotic control, that is control merely to please the whim or fancy of the individual or groups who direct the citizen for their own advantage. Civil and natural liberty is a freedom limited only by laws established on behalf of the welfare of the community or the state.

"It is evident, therefore, that liberty begins in the freedom of the individual from selfish control or exploitation on the part of another or others.

"If an autocrat or a plutocrat controls, directs or regiments the actions of an individual, that individual has lost his liberty to that extent.

"However, if an individual is doing that which interferes with the freedom or comfort of another, his liberty has invaded the field of license. That is, I have liberty to swing my fist around as I please as long as I do not come too close to you or your face. Then it is your right to object. I have exceeded my liberty rights.

"If you examine the popular cries of liberty today you will find that they are not that at all, but are invasions in the realm of license and therefore for the public good, they must be controlled and adjudged by the state. They tell you that the principle of licensing is fundamentally inconsistent with British traditions and customs. That is a most extravagant, untrue and unwarranted statement. Tell me what profession of today is not licensed. Lawyers, teachers and preachers are all licensed. It does not interfere with their liberty in the slightest, except to protect the public.

"Doctors, druggists, chemists, opticians and others are required to have a license. Is that against British tradition and custom?

"It is rather amusing and most surprising to hear of lawyers and of preachers objecting to licensing as un-British, when in their own profession they are most insistent upon its enforcement.

"The previous government heard no complaint regarding the licensing of gasoline stations, and not only that but the limiting of the number.

"We are told that it is alright to license picture shows, films and billboard advertising to protect the morals of our people. We cannot allow the individual to show on billboards or screens anything he desires to show. But it is un-British and unwarranted, say they, to license newspapers and publishing houses or prevent them from publishing what they like. It would be against the liberty of the press. You must not use prevention with them. You can only use cure. If the press blackens the character of a man or publishes gross misrepresentations you can go to court about it and, if you can, get damages. Why not do the same with the moving picture houses, and billboards and doctors and druggists.

"Surely it is evident that a license is for the purpose of preventing wrong and injustice when it touches the welfare of others, rather than curing faults already done. There is no need of licensing occupations or businesses which do not corrupt nor interfere with the welfare of others. The wild statement that the present government intends to license farmers and house-maids shows the foolish misunderstanding of the whole principle.

"Why should anyone object to a license who is conducting his business or occupation for the welfare of the people?"

He declared that exploitation of the public should and would cease and while the government had every intention of protecting the people by licensing where such action was deemed advisable, there was no thought of interfering with individual liberty in the carrying out of this act.

---

22 ABERHART SHOULD RESIGN

Calgary Herald
March 23, 1937

"The fair thing for Premier Aberhart to do is to step down and allow the Social Credit members of the Alberta Legislature to choose a new premier, determined to implement fully the social credit program," declares P.J. Rowe, Independent Social Credit member for Athabaska, in a statement released here today.

Mr. Rowe issued a flat denial to the statement that he would oust Mr. Aberhart from the premiership and either take the post himself or appoint another. He repeated his earlier statements that social credit had made no progress under Mr. Aberhart and that there could be no real hope of progress while he continued as leader, but he emphasized the point that "whoever may be chosen to succeed Mr. Aberhart will be chosen by the elected members of the Alberta legislature."

Mr. Rowe's statement is as follows:

"That the Social Credit movement is not dependent on any one individual is one point upon which I am in thorough accord with Premier Aberhart. Social credit is in fact the demand of a free people for deliverance from economic bondage; it is for that very reason that I have not hesitated to inform the people themselves of the true conditions and the lack of progress in Alberta.

"To the statement that I would oust Mr. Aberhart from the premiership and either take the job myself or appoint another, I cannot answer other than with an absolute denial that I ever uttered any such words.

"I did say, and I repeat, that it is my considered opinion that social credit has made no progress under the leadership of Mr. Aberhart, and that it is my firm conviction that there can be no real hope of progress whilst he continues as the leader.

"As to the choice of a new leader, it must of necessity be conceded that whoever may be chosen to succeed Mr. Aberhart will be chosen by the elected members of the legislature. That is their business and theirs only. I am not concerned with any leader. My interest is to see that social credit is implemented in Alberta. I do believe that strong leadership and technical advice are both essential without any further delay."

23 CONFLICT OCCURS OVER BUDGET

Calgary Herald
March 23, 1937

The provincial government is prepared to call a general election within sixty days if the insurgent group on the government side succeeds in its reported plan to defeat the budget on the floor of the House unless it is withdrawn by Provincial Treasurer Solon Low, it was reported in official circles this morning.

It was announced definitely this morning that the budget would not be withdrawn, and that the government was prepared to face any challenge which might come, either from their own members or from the combined Liberal and Conservative opposition.

Legislative halls buzzed with gossip this morning when it became known that the insurgent group had held another private meeting on Monday evening and that a new social credit bill, based on the Douglas social credit plan, had been drafted by a caucus committee composed almost entirely of members of the insurgent group.

Overtures have been made to Hon. Solon Low to introduce the bill in the House as a government measure, and the provincial treasurer is reported to have agreed to introduce the bill on one condition only—and that is that government members vote for adoption of the budget as it now stands.

Members of the planning group argue that if the budget is adopted as introduced in the House it will not be possible to put the social credit plan into operation. They state that the budget, therefore, must be withdrawn and a new budget drafted to dovetail with the social credit plan, must be placed before the members.

The provincial treasurer has emphatically refused, however, to withdraw his budget, and the situation is deadlocked.

Asked what would happen if members of the government side lined up with the opposition to defeat the budget and succeeded in outvoting the government, an official said that the premier would have no alternative but to advise the lieutenant-governor-in-council that the government was prepared to go to the people at the earliest possible date.

"When the private members who are interested in the new bill are confronted with the seriousness of any move which would result in the estimates not being approved by the end of the month, I am quite sure that they will withdraw their opposition to the present budget," a cabinet minister stated this morning.

"If the estimates are not passed by the end of the month it means that governmental machinery will come to a full stop."

In the meantime, the insurgent group is keeping silent about its plans.

"Wait and see" was the answer given by one of the members this morning when questioned concerning the report that the group would "filibuster" the budget debate until the end of the month, if the government did not withdraw the budget proper.

Some are openly sceptical concerning the reported action which might be taken by the insurgent group to force an issue in the House.

"Just talk," one government member stated. He does not belong to the group.

"The boys are ready to make an issue of it," another member said. He belongs to the insurgent group.

"We want real social credit and there is only one way to get it and that is to see that the new social credit bill is approved," another member said.

"Even if it means the resignation of the premier," the member was asked.

"This movement is bigger than any one man. If anyone tries to block it in any way, they must get out, no matter who it is," was the reply.

Asked if the crisis would come this afternoon when the House re-convenes, the member said that he was not prepared to say just when it would come.

"One thing is certain, however—it is going to come soon."

Edmonton Journal
March 24, 1937

Differences within the ranks of the Social Credit party were partially composed at a protracted caucus in the legislative buildings, Tuesday night.

Budget terms which had been attacked by R.E. Ansley, M.L.A. for Leduc, in the house earlier in the day and which had been criticized by various other government members, were endorsed with not more than 12 of the 49 members present voting against them.

Mr. Ansley was acting general secretary of the Alberta Social Credit league during its organization last year, leaving the post when a permanent official was appointed at the January convention here. He also was a member of the government's special planning committee which had the assistance of John Hargrave, British Social Credit leader, in drafting a plan for Alberta during the winter.

Government concessions, said by a member to have been given in return for budget support were:

(1) The bringing of Major C.H. Douglas, British Social Credit founder and former adviser to the Alberta government, or "some other adviser" to assist in preparing an Alberta Social Credit plan.

(2) The dropping of the contentious bill to license all trades, businesses, industries and occupations and to provide for price fixing.

Premier Aberhart on Wednesday confirmed the report that the new business licensing and price-fixing bills are to be dropped by the government.

"Will the bills be proceeded with?" the premier was asked.

"No," he replied.

Asked as to reports that the bills were being dropped because of a saw-off between the government and insurgent forces, the premier denied this was the case.

"There was no saw-off," he said. "It was the feeling that the bills should not be proceeded with, and that was not based upon other considerations."

The premier said it was not the intention to hold a sitting of the house on Good Friday, but there might be a sitting on Easter Monday. He said he was mainly concerned now with action on the budget and passing of the estimates before March 31.

"The debt adjustment legislation and the Social Credit bill will be brought down in due course immediately after the budget is passed," said the premier.

Rev. Peter Dawson, speaker of the legislature and caucus chairman, also refused to make a statement.

"I don't think we will see anything brought in at this session to pay basic dividends," said a member of the caucus Wednesday.

From 8:45 p.m. until after midnight, the caucus remained in session to thresh out the differences of opinion and set the Social Credit ship in smoother water for the balance of the session.

Some members of the government, particularly Hon. N.E. Tanner, minister of lands and mines, urged the necessity of adopting the budget, it is learned. This confirmed reports earlier in the day that the government would stand pat on its budget, though some Social Credit members had criticized its orthodox features.

One of the big factors in bringing about approval of the budget was the necessity of voting appropriations for seed grain relief this spring, it is claimed. Authorization for the province's share of seed grain relief costs is in the budget, under "agricultural relief."

Budget supporters pointed out, it is reported, that mortgage companies were concerned over the possible action to be taken by the province and might not agree to participate in regard to providing seed grain relief if the budget were not passed. It is understood that the amount involved in seed grain relief is around $1,600,000, slightly more than the cost in 1936.

Decision to "kill" the licensing and price control bills was regarded as a victory for those who have expressed strong criticisms of these measures. Recently it was rumored that the licensing bill in particular, which has aroused a storm of protest, might be thrown out by the caucus.

25 THE AWAKENING

Calgary Herald
March 24, 1937

The amazing expedient of threatening closure in the House to cut off discussion of the budget by its own Social Credit supporter, this was the measure of the government's real strength in the caucus at Edmonton last night. The very moderate speech of R.E. Ansley at yesterday's sitting of the legislature revealed a situation that has been developing for many weeks. For those who sincerely believed, and sincerely endorsed, the fluent promises of 1935, it is a tragic situation but one by one the Social Credit members of the legislature are facing the fact that their leaders have done nothing about Social Credit and almost literally know nothing about Social Credit.

Within the last few months it has dawned on these members, one by one, that the government's attitude toward even them has been one of evasion. Within the last few weeks they have realized that the so-called preparation for a new economic order consisted of just one bluff after another—a moderately adroit effort to dangle the greatest number of carrots before a dwindling number of faithful noses.

In very restrained language Mr. Ansley yesterday afternoon shattered all pretense that these misgivings have not been spreading among government supporters. In less restrained language, at last night's caucus, his fellow-doubters asked the government what they were to tell their constituents, and the government's response in part was a quiet intimation that an undue airing of such doubts on the floor of the House could be met with the closure. And perhaps that is also the measure of free speech and free thought within the Aberhart organization.

To back this up, it strenuously protested that if the budget were delayed beyond the end of the fiscal year, government machinery would come to a halt in Alberta. There would be a cessation of relief grants, a blockade of seed grain loans, and—quite incidentally of course—no provision for the $1,800 sessional indemnity to members of the legislature. All of which was excellent politics for the moment, but only for the moment.

For it completely overlooks the fact that delay in passing a budget is by no means an unheard of situation among governments, and one that is quite easily met by a temporary vote of funds to carry on with. And to refuse such a vote would simply place the government in the position of sabotaging its own administration—at the expense of the people.

This afternoon the House is meeting in an atmosphere of crises. It would be idle to speculate on possible developments an hour ahead of time. But of all the possibilities, the most dramatic and most damaging to the prestige of the present cabinet are the very two that it has itself adumbrated.

To take the responsibility of blocking relief grants and seed loans would be to invite a political lynching.

To apply the gag to its own supporters because they happen to be in a critical mood would be political hari-kiri [*sic*]—a little slower, a little more spectacular, outwardly a little more honorable. But death just the same.

26 GOVERNMENT TO RESIGN?

Calgary Herald
March 25, 1937

Social Credit insurgents will seek the support of their constituents at emergency meetings which will be held over the Easter holidays, if time will allow, it was stated this morning.

Coupled with this announcement came the report that the government would resign immediately if it is defeated on the budget vote on the floor of the legislature.

Wednesday's afternoon events in the House, when the government was defeated by a vote of 27 to 25, proved conclusively that there is no "saw-off" between the insurgents and the government and that it will be a fight to a finish.

Insurgent leaders stated this morning that the revolt was not merely an attempt to embarrass the government.

It was the only way, they contended, in which private members could bring to the attention of their supporters the fact that government had made little or no attempt to carry out pre-election promises by introducing a social credit plan.

They stated that they would continue their attack upon the budget until it is withdrawn, or until it comes to a vote on the floor of the House.

"We are prepared to defeat the government, if possible, on this question of principle," one of the leaders said.

Reports that the government may resign even before the budget vote came gained credence this morning.

---

27 CABINET MAY SEEK $3,000,000

Calgary Herald
March 27, 1937

Confronted with the gravest crisis since taking office, with insurgent members showing surprising strength, Alberta's Social Credit government has decided to hold up the budget now before the legislature.

Hon. Solon Low, provincial treasurer, today confirmed reports that he will present a resolution to the House on Monday asking for approval of provisional estimates.

Just what amount will be proposed as a provisional vote has not been decided, Mr. Low stated.

In other quarters, it is understood that the government will ask for a vote of approximately $3,000,000 to meet expenditures for a period of two months at least.

"Does it mean that the budget is being withdrawn?" Mr. Low was asked.

"It is being held up, or suspended temporarily," the minister admitted.

"The business of this province must go on," Mr. Low stated.

With regard to the amount to be voted, Mr. Low said that was a matter for the legislative assembly to decide.

The biggest thing to consider now was that there would be no disruption in the business of the province, he said.

Need of immediate action confronts the government as it is necessary for some authorization to be given for any expenditures to be made after Wednesday, March 31.

Should the insurgent filibuster, which continued this week, be maintained successfully on Monday, the government faces the prospect of having no authority to spend any public funds after Wednesday, which is the end of the fiscal year. It is to avert such a contingency that the provincial treasurer is proposing that the House pass provisional estimates to enable the government to carry on while it is debating the budget.

In insurgent ranks, reports of the government move to secure the passage of provisional estimates brought firm declarations that there would be strong opposition until the government agreed to the acceptance of the social credit bills, which the insurgents have their hearts set on as being a prime requisite to joint action with the government supporters.

It was also indicated that there would be strong opposition to the motion of which notice has been given by Premier Aberhart, to bring in the closure on the budget debate.

Should the House agree to the passing of provisional estimates, it was suggested that the premier might withdraw the closure motion and allow the budget debate to proceed without objection.

---

28 S.C. INSURGENTS TO DEFEAT GOVERNMENT?

Edmonton Journal
March 29, 1937

While eager spectators, sensing the drama of the hour, lined up outside the legislative buildings and jammed into every available gallery seat, sittings of the legislature were resumed at 3:00 p.m. Monday as insurgent and "loyal" factions within the world's first Social Credit government prepared for a definite test of strength on the floor of the house.

Insurgent Social Credit members Monday announced their determination to defeat the government's scheme for voting provisional estimates pending passage of the budget.

Meantime it was learned that the government, making what observers called an 11th-hour move to "outsmart" the rebel forces who have been calling for immediate steps toward establishment of Social Credit, had prepared an answer to those demands.

Proposed by Hon. Solon Low, provincial treasurer, a motion was placed on the order paper for Monday's sitting, providing for the appointment of a five-man commission under the Social Credit Measures act to investigate and report upon a Social Credit plan for the province.

Though insurgent spokesmen insisted that victory was near and the defeat of the government inevitable, Premier Aberhart declared shortly before the sitting started that he "will stand or fall" by the budget now before the house.

As Monday's debate began, rebel leaders said confidently they had enough support assured to defeat "whenever it is submitted" the motion for provisional estimates.

Public interest in the crisis rose Monday to an unparalleled pitch as hundreds of persons, more than half of whom were women, thronged the steps of the legislative buildings in an effort to seize the few precious seats waiting for them in the spectators' gallery. Scores of these were in line long before noon. Some brought lunches as they started their three-hour vigil.

As opening time neared officials arranged to install loud speakers for the benefit of the crowd outside the building.

"We plan to defeat the motion for provisional estimates whenever it is submitted and have the necessary support assured," said one prominent insurgent before the day's sitting of the legislature opened.

Whether he would be prepared to withdraw the closure motion to end discussion of the debate, of which he gave notice last Wednesday, the premier was not prepared to say.

He had indicated Sunday in Calgary that withdrawal of the closure plan might be expected.

"What action will be taken if the motion to pass provisional estimates is defeated?" the Premier was asked.

"The debate would continue and we would go to a vote on the budget," said the premier.

"This matter will have to be settled on the floor of the house," he declared.

The premier refused to confirm reports that he had been approached by a delegation of insurgent members and urged to resign on the understanding that he would be named Alberta's official representative to the coronation.

"I don't know anything about it," he stated.

Indications early Monday were that insur-gent members were determined to come to grips with the government as soon as the house opened at 3:00 p.m.

It was declared by insurgents that they had at least 30 members in support of their stand against the government.

These members held that it was no time for half-way measures and that complete surrender of the government to their demands was the only move that would save the situation.

Insurgents were firm in their opposition to passing the budget or voting provisional estimates until the legislation providing for the establishment of a Social Credit program in this province had been introduced.

A resolution providing for voting of provisional estimates by the house owing to the new fiscal year opening Thursday, had been placed on the order paper for Monday's sitting by Hon. Solon Low, provincial treasurer.

This proposed that the house vote interim supply for a period of three months. It is figured that this would mean a vote of around $5,000,000 as the total expenditure proposed under the 1937-38 budget is $21,000,000.

29 THEY BOTH WIN

Calgary Herald
March 31, 1937

One of the strangest situations in Canadian parliamentary history has just arrived in Edmonton at a temporary solution that is equally strange.

It has not often occurred that a Canadian government has found its life in danger by a barrage from its own followers. That these followers should be taking it to task for being recreant to its promises is even more picturesque. And that the head of this government should respond by attempting to apply the gag to his own party in the House is not merely unique but bizarre.

Quite in keeping with such a fantastic crisis is the fact that it could be tided over by the Cabinet's acceptance of a public dragooning on the floor of the House and consent to hold up the budget itself pending compliance with the demands of a rebellious element.

Doubtless today's position has one (purely political) advantage. Both sides will find themselves able to rejoice in it. The insurgents having forced the government to capitulate can claim a moral victory. And the government having, by capitulation, bought off the insurgents can and will claim that it remains undefeated. But whether the resulting position should be described as armistice, stalemate, deadlock or reconciliation no one, even on the floor of the House itself, seems yet to know.

---

30 FURTHER CONFLICT WITHIN THE RANKS

Edmonton Journal
April 1, 1937

While "insurgent" leaders claimed Thursday that Premier Aberhart has given an assurance that he would voluntarily place his resignation before the Social Credit caucus Wednesday night, the premier denied Thursday that he had made any such promise.

The caucus, which was called by the premier, ended at 1:10 a.m. Thursday without a decision.

"Is it true, as insurgents claim, that you gave the assurance," the premier was asked.

"I did not give any assurance of the kind," he replied. "I told the member who came to see me that I would not bargain. If they (insurgents) wanted to bring something in, they could do so in the house."

It had been claimed by insurgent leaders that they had the understanding that if they withdrew opposition to the third reading of the interim budget on Wednesday, the premier would place his resignation, which also would carry that of the cabinet, before the caucus.

"A representative of a small committee called on the premier Wednesday and discussed the situation. He then advised the premier that he should resign in the interests of the Social Credit movement. The premier was informed that otherwise, our group of members would be prepared to defeat the interim budget," said this prominent insurgent.

Insurgent leaders claim that their group attended the caucus because of the understanding that the premier's resignation would be placed before the members for action.

"We said that we were prepared to co-operate if the resignation were placed before the caucus. That assurance was given by the premier," said an insurgent leader.

In insurgent circles Thursday, there were beliefs that a showdown would come on the floor of the house if not elsewhere.

"Something may happen Thursday. You had better be ready," said one S.C. member.

Just what the next move would be was uncertain, as political circles remained in a turmoil. It was regarded as possible that important developments might take place any time.

The caucus was called by Premier Aberhart himself who addressed the members briefly at 9:30 p.m., stating that he wished to know the feeling of the caucus in view of opposition expressed to him in the house. He said that he and his cabinet would await word from the caucus in his office.

The "insurgents" and "loyalists" then discussed whether non-confidence should be voted in the administration. The caucus ended at 1:10 a.m. without a decision being reached, it was reported.

"There is no statement whatever to make," said Hon. Peter Dawson, speaker of the house, who acted as chairman, when seen afterward.

"I have nothing whatever to say," said Premier Aberhart as he emerged from the meeting of the cabinet.

All members of the cabinet were present at the meeting in his office with the exception of Hon. E.C. Manning, provincial secretary, and Hon. J.W. Hugill, K.C. attorney-general. Members of the ministry kept silent concerning the situation.

"You can say definitely that the government has not resigned. There is nothing more that I can say," declared one private member after the caucus.

Some members of the insurgent group were reported to be firm in the demand that reorganization of the cabinet was essential. Whether they would go to the extent of voting non-confidence if the question arose in the house was unsettled.

General opinion veered to the belief that rebellious members were hopeful of the government taking the voluntary step of resigning, which would prove a peaceful solution and avoid making the breach in the ranks wider still.

The caucus call resulted in a flood of rumors that the government had decided to resign.

Insurgent and other members hurried to the legislative buildings, anticipating some important announcement.

Shortly after 9:00 p.m., the members were called into caucus. The premier arrived late due to attendance at the teachers' convention.

From time to time, private members came out of the caucus room but declined to talk about the developments.

"They are just threshing things out and getting nowhere," said one member.

"We have had a long discussion but there are no developments and nothing to announce," said a prominent insurgent.

"The premier asked us to consider the whole situation and endeavor to reach a decision. To enable us to do so freely he said that he and other members of the cabinet would stay away from the meeting," said this member.

During the long drawn out session, a committee of the Social Credit members drafted two questions which it was suggested that the caucus should vote upon.

One was: Do you want William Aberhart? The other was: Whom do you want for your new leader?

When these questions were put before the caucus, it was learned from a member who was present, there was strong objection to a vote being taken. It was felt that it would be unfair to the principals concerned. The upshot was that no vote was taken on the question and no other votes were taken during the evening.

Finally, the premier was advised the caucus could not reach a decision as to what course should be taken concerning the ministry.

31   RESTRAINING INFLUENCES

Calgary Herald
April 5, 1937

While there is little doubt as to the sincerity of the insurgent movement to get rid of Premier Aberhart, it has become fairly evident in the past few days that the "rebels" will stop short of forcing a complete showdown. They are not keen on precipitating a general election.

The Premier has stated after a week of severe buffeting from the malcontents in the party's ranks that he and his cabinet will resign only if defeated on the floor of the house. This is his position in the face of rebuffs sufficient to compel any other head of a government in the British Empire to hand in his resignation in order to preserve his self-respect. His authority has been openly flouted, his budget has been side-tracked by the insurgents, his veracity has been questioned in the legislature, but he clings to the emoluments of office, and his ministerial colleagues sit tight with him. They are even prepared to allow the insurgent wing to name a new Commission which in large measure will dictate the policies and course of the government. In other words, they will yield even the pretence of governing.

The reason is obvious why the rebellious element want a new Premier but not another election. All the government members owe their election to the fact that they were the chosen of Mr. Aberhart and his small nomination committee. Constituencies were not allowed to make the final choices. This unique method of selecting candidates left a legacy of bitterness in its wake. The rejected aspirants for preferment in 1935 have a real grievance against the Premier and the sitting members and at least some of them may be eagerly awaiting another nomination day to advance their claims.

A certain percentage of the sitting members might not win a renomination and, if they did so, would be confronted by opposition within their own ranks. And the exuberant enthusiasm for a new cause which swept over the province in 1935 must be considerably deflated by nineteen months of disappointing administration. The old battle cries of two years ago have lost much of their potency. And if the dynamic leader, who was regarded as a Messiah two years ago, were dethroned, the men who brought about his overthrow would assuredly find a divided party in their constituencies and be without the support of the weekly political broadcasts from the Bible Institute.

It is considerations like these, and the crude but timely proposal that the pay of members should be raised, that lend a suggestion of shadow-boxing to the lengthy insurgent caucuses and manoeuvering in Edmonton in the past few days.

32 THE SOCIAL CREDIT BOARD

Calgary Herald
April 12, 1937

Through legislation creating a Social Credit Board, consisting of five back-benchers, the Aberhart Government is seeking to divest itself of responsibility for the introduction of Social Credit in this province. It is trying to take the onus off its own shoulders and place it on a group which the Premier himself passed over when he sought men for ministerial duty.

While these five private members engage in the herculean task of trying to find honest-to-goodness Social Credit legislation in all parts of the world, and of studying the economic conditions in Alberta, Premier Aberhart and his cabinet colleagues will twiddle their thumbs and continue to draw their big salaries. No doubt they visualize a peaceful three months ahead during the legislative recess while the members of the new Board try to make good where they have failed.

It is an extraordinary spectacle of ministerial responsibility being delegated to humble followers. However, the latter are to be rewarded by eight dollars a day each and expenses. The taxpayers will be called on to foot the bill. Diogenes in far-off times went out with his lantern to find an honest man. How much easier was his task than the odyssey of Mr. MacLachan of Coronation and his colleagues in which they will seek a real Social Credit "expert", unless they succeed in inducing Major Douglas to come to Alberta, and even he seems to leave something to be desired in the way of performance. He has talked a lot and written more about the theories that bear his name, but he has never attempted to put them into practice anywhere in the world. He has, however, advised against direct political action, and that is what the Aberhart Government has been attempting to apply during the past nineteen months.

The act appointing the new Social Credit Board takes away from the government itself powers formally granted to it by the legislature for the purpose of introducing a Social Credit system. These powers are not vested in the new Board which can in turn appoint a permanent commission of three members to make Social Credit work. This would seem to remove the responsibility a long way from Premier Aberhart, the man who landed the province in its present predicament. But disgruntled Social Credit followers and the opponents of the government will not have it that way. They will place the onus squarely on the broad shoulders of the Premier and keep it there until the day of reckoning.

---

33 PREMIER WIELDS BIG STICK AGAIN

Edmonton Journal
April 20, 1937

The ultimatum delivered by Mr. Aberhart on Sunday evening puts up to his insurgent followers a very definite choice. They were told that they "should either stand behind the government or cross the floor as another party in opposition." He asked that constituency groups instruct their members which course they were to take, as he regarded as evident that "there should be no serious criticism of the government from the government side of the house."

It is impossible to believe that the Social Credit members who have criticized the government so strongly will, when presented with this alternative, fail to reply that they prefer to go into outright opposition. They have been accused of being prompted by enemies of Social Credit to take the stand that they did in the legislature. Mrs. Gostick of Calgary, in an address in that city on Thursday, stated that their attacks had been organized by the "financial powers." They have a right to resent such a charge as they made it clear that attitude was due simply to their having lost patience with the government's delay in implementing the pledge on which it came into office.

In view of the way in which Mr. Aberhart has recently yielded to the insurgents, it was surprising to have him use the language of defiance that he did on Sunday. As a result of their revolt he and his cabinet associates have surrendered to a committee of private members the task of initiating a Social Credit system. Thus the government has ceased to function, so far as the work that it was formed to do is concerned.

Under these circumstances it is hard to see how the premier can expect to wield successfully the big stick which he is now flourishing once again. Whatever is behind his latest step, it is an unique one for a leader to take. Where differences have arisen in a party in the past its head has not sought to put an end to these by inviting a group of members elected as his supporters to join the opposition if they cannot see eye to eye with him. But we have grown accustomed by this time to unprecedented political happenings in Alberta.

SECTION III

The Press, the Courts, and the Constitution, 1936-1938

1936-1938

1 STATEMENTS ON SOCIAL CREDIT CRITICIZED

Albertan
January 6, 1936

Criticizing an article appearing in a national magazine on the subject of Social Credit, rapping the press of Canada in general, and stating a Social Credit daily newspaper in Alberta might be necessary, Premier William Aberhart addressed the congregation of the Calgary Prophetic Bible Institute Sunday afternoon. The address, the first since the premier's return from his vacation at the Pacific coast, was broadcast.

Opening his remarks, the premier called attention to the fact that the newspapers were making fun of the institute's Sunday afternoon meetings and broadcasts, and calling them "political meetings." "I hope they listen to them sometimes, and I hope they get saved when they do," remarked Premier Aberhart, amid laughter.

The premier then launched into a reply to the editor of a Canadian magazine, who had written an article in the last issue of the magazine on "What of Social Credit?" following a trip to Alberta.

"How on earth can any man make 'a thorough examination of the system' and yet write what this man did?" asked the premier.

The premier took particular exception to the statements in the article that he owned radio broadcasting station CFCN which was, according to the article, housed in the Prophetic Bible Institute. He pointed out that he did not own the station, that the transmitter was located at Strathmore, and that the studios were in a local office building. "I wish I did own it, but I don't," he said. "I have no control aside from a regular contract."

He also took exception to the article's statement that there was a 'rumor' that he had made a lot of money out of the Bible Institute. "Over and over again," said the premier, "I have asserted that I have made no money out of this institute. There is an auditor's statement issued every year."

Referring to repeated attacks on himself, Premier Aberhart said he "had now a rhinocerous hide and was now developing Abyssinian feet."

"For any Canadian magazine to make such an unwarranted attack is unfair," said the speaker. "I hope they will come through and give this radio station a true statement."

"The press is becoming a nuisance. The people of the world are beginning to realize that they will have to own and control their own press. We don't want to go into the publishing business but we won't be afraid to go into it. If some of these days I tell you that Social Crediters are going to have a daily paper I hope you'll support it," he said. Applause greeted his last remark.

Arriving for his vacation at Vancouver, hoping to get a rest, he had no sooner got off the train than newspapermen were "on his tail" seeking some statement to distort, said the premier. "I'm glad there won't be any newspapers in Heaven," he said.

2 PENALTY OF FAME

Edmonton Journal
January 14, 1936

Mr. Aberhart says the press "is becoming a nuisance," suggests to his Alberta followers a time may come when Social Credit forces in that province may need a daily paper of their own. Perhaps against that contingency they had better save up their basic dividends—"if, as and when."

Premier Aberhart is paying the penalty of his fame. A few months ago he stormed the forces of the established parties and achieved a sensational victory—the first electoral victory of consequence ever secured by Social Credit economists. Immediately he was a world figure. People everywhere either hailed him as the prophet of a new order, or wanted to know something more about his theories and intentions. He became front-page news, and people eager to hail an economic messiah waited on his lightest word. They still do, though possibly with less confidence.

Now Mr. Aberhart pleads for time, for freedom from the sort of attention that elevated him to his present eminence and responsibility. He complains that he is "besieged" by reporters. He complains that a magazine writer "escaped legal penalties" by qualifying a report about him with the phrase, "rumor said," although if the statement was libelous the qualifying phrase was no safeguard, as every newspaper knows. And he says he "may have to do something severe" in the next few weeks—possibly something to assure himself freedom from comment and criticism.

It is pitiful and rather childish. As a figure of more even than national significance Mr. Aberhart cannot escape public attention, and so long as comment is confined to his administration and his policies he has no real grievance. He must not deny to others the very freedom of speech and action that permitted him to secure the post from which now he looks down upon the common reporter as a public nuisance.

3 SOCIAL CREDIT PARTY'S DAILY ORGAN

Edmonton Journal
January 16, 1936

At one time most Canadian newspapers were party organs. So it is nothing new in the business of newspaper publishing to have the Calgary Albertan converted into "the official organ of the Alberta Social Credit party." This is what it announced yesterday morning it is henceforth to be.

No one has any right to criticize the supporters of a political organization if, with the object of advancing its interests, they launch out on such a venture. What use they make of their own money is their affair. But it has been almost invariably found that the party organ is of no advantage to the party and also that the investment is not a good one for the stockholders. This is why the great majority of the newspapers of the dominion have ceased to be in that category. Though they have their political opinions, they are conducted quite independently of any party.

"By winning the Albertan's allegiance," that newspaper says, "the proponents of Social Credit implement one of the conditions which Major Douglas stated to be vital: access to press and radio." Mr. Aberhart declares that "this action will help Social Crediters implement the requirements of Major Douglas in his interim report regarding the radio station and the press."

But what Major Douglas recommended was "the systematic provision of a news circulation system, under the unchallengeable control of the province, particularly in regard to radio facilities of sufficient power to cover a wide geographical area." This proposal to have the province go into the circulation of news, evidently for the purpose of influencing opinion in favor of the policies which the major advocates, was described at the time in these columns as "too much in line with what has been done in Germany and Russia to be to the liking of Canadian citizens."

The province is not undertaking anything of the kind now. There is no mention of provincial funds being used in connection with the enterprise.

Practically all Alberta newspapers opposed the Social Credit movement. But they have given their space freely to presenting the claims that it has made on public support, as they were bound to do in the proper discharge of their duty to their readers. Nor is there any reasonable ground for complaint in regard to the treatment that the government has received at their hands. So, while they will not be at all disposed to challenge that party's action in securing a daily organ of its own, they must dispute the contention that the step was necessary in order to give the people of the province accurate and complete information in regard to Social Credit and governmental policies. This they have had all along.

4 ABERHART SCORES PRESS REGULATIONS

Edmonton Journal
February 5, 1936

The Alberta government will give a sympathetic ear to any organized appeal by newspapers for relief from the "press bills" passed at the 1935 session as amendments to the libel and slander act, it was stated Wednesday by Premier Aberhart.

"I do not believe that those bills were handled in the right way," the premier said. "I do not believe that they were just, or that their objective was correct.

"There is a necessity for some kind of regulation of what newspapers print, but I believe that if publishers themselves came to the government with concrete proposals we could draft a plan which would enable us to amend or rescind last year's press bills."

Last year's amendments prohibited publication of any evidence, details of claims, or any other particulars concerning divorce cases or other court hearings dealing with family matters. At the same time, publication of proceedings in court chambers was banned.

---

5 MR. ABERHART AND THE PRESS

Albertan
September 15, 1936

The premier dropped a hint on Sunday more definite than he has dropped before that the licencing of Alberta newspapers might have to be considered. The outcry of "Hands off the press!' has been raised even more punctually than we had anticipated. There are times when such a cry might well go up, but the judge of when to raise it is not the press itself—particularly that section which has most need of being controlled. We are not afraid of that word "controlled" nor have any apology for using it.

Because every radio station in the country operates under a license which can be cancelled if the station persistently offends against the canons of good taste, will it be said that the radio is "controlled"? It is a well known fact that it is not. Are motion pictures "controlled" because they have to pass a censor before they are shown publicly? Decent radio and films have nothing to fear at the hands of licensing boards. What, then is biting the newspapers that call out so loudly about "the liberty of the press"?

What is the liberty of the press? Whatever it may be does not allow the press to speak maliciously, directly or by innuendo, either of private citizens or public men. Fair comment on a matter of public interest is not libellous in the eyes of the law, nor is it going to be here suggested that the comment in most of the editorial columns has been generally speaking, anything but fair. The unfair comment has rather been the comment the newswriter has put into the mouth of the man on the street and the headlines whose writers have put their own mistaken interpretation into the day's news. That is simply malicious and malice is the essence of libel, for which a private citizen has recourse to the courts.

Freedom of the press is one of those "British institutions" of which we boast. It is one of the things for which, we say with pride, our fathers bled and all that sort of thing. But when our fathers bled for it (if they did) it was that thereby the people should secure their own liberties through their press; not that the press should keep them from them. Sometimes when we read newspapers monotoning about their liberty we think they forget that liberty was accorded them not for their advantage but for their readers'. If the press abuses the liberty which is its by usage it is the people for whose benefit the liberty of the press exists who suffer. Liberty of the press is not something which the press has secured for itself. It is only another of those democratic abstractions of the same order as justice, equality of opportunity and so forth. It is something to be enjoyed, like those, in proportion as the subject deserves it.

---

6 DICTATORS AND THE PRESS

Calgary Herald
May 4, 1937

The dictators of Italy and Germany, Mussolini and Hitler, have decreed that a free press is inimical to autocracy, but both are profiting personally from the newspaper profession. Mussolini is the owner of the well-known Italian newspaper, Popolo D'Italia, and he has turned it into a lucrative enterprise by the simple expedient of making it the mouthpiece of government pronouncements. Whenever his personal newspaper contains an important statement, Mussolini orders all newspapers in Italy to print the following announcement: "The Popolo D'Italia today carries an important article on such and such a subject." These newspapers cannot reproduce the statement until the following day, so Il Duce's newspaper is bought by the hundreds of thousands and the dictator reaps the profits.

Hitler follows a similar system in Germany, but he goes farther by a system of intimidation applied to business firms. If they do not advertise in his newspaper, they are suspected of lukewarmness for the Nazi regime. The result is that the Hitler organ is a very prosperous enterprise.

On a smaller scale something of the same nature was attempted in Alberta by Premier Aberhart. Not only did he boycott one Calgary newspaper, but on Sunday and week days he urged his followers to purchase stock and advertise in another local newspaper. However, this is not Italy or Germany, and Aberhart is neither a Hitler nor a Mussolini, and the scheme failed even as social credit has failed.

---

7 IMPLEMENTATION OF S.C. PROGRAM

Edmonton Journal
August 3, 1937

Declarations that the government was ready to take definite steps to implement Social Credit, came from the first speakers in the debate on the speech from the throne in the legislature Tuesday.

"The people, through their M.L.A.'s [sic] have been exercising their democratic right to press for results. That is why we are here—to take definite action to implement their demands," said A.J. Hooke, eloquent S.C. member for Red Deer and former insurgent in moving the reply to the throne speech.

Shortly after, E.O. Duke, S.C., Rocky Mountain House who during the "split" in the S.C. ranks last spring was a "loyal" supporter of the government, declared: "We now are ready to take active steps to implement the definitely expressed will of the people at the last election in August, 1935."

Mr. Hooke remarked that in perusing the speech from the throne, he could find very little of a definite nature of the action to be taken at this session.

"However, it does make some mention of endeavoring to remedy some of the conditions which are still distressing our people. One of these is the increasingly difficult relief problem" said Mr. Hooke.

"I am firmly convinced that the problem of relief is a national one and not one which can be handled by each small locality. I trust the committee chosen at the last session has some recommendations to make of a definite nature toward centralized relief," he said.

Another distressing problem was that of increased taxation, said Mr. Hooke.

"The only solution, I believe, is the changing of our economic structure. The other so-called solution is borrowing, thus mortgaging our children for the future. That has been amply proven to be ridiculous.

"The borrowings of the past are the cause of the high taxes of today. I trust that the new Social Credit legislation will be the solution to the tax problem," he said.

Problem of tax arrears was a tremendous one with the municipalities, he said. Situation was such that the farmers could not work out back taxes as the council had hypothecated them to the banks. The government could not give the municipalities a grant and consequently little or no work was done on the roads.

"I have wondered if some arrangement could be made whereby the banks liberate their hold upon the tax arrears so that the farmer may work out his indebtedness on the roads, the council in turn to guarantee to pay to the banks as large a portion as possible of the current taxes.

"The farmer would begin to see a way out and make a better effort to pay his current taxes, the banks would be paid back and the province would get its much needed market roads," said Mr. Hooke.

Later, the member declared that "the legislative assembly exists to implement the will of the people. The people of this province have demanded in no uncertain terms that they get a dividend of $25 a month and a lower cost to live. These are the results they have instructed us to obtain—and this is their will."

"Our people must be taught what is the proper action for them to take to end this distress. We must teach the people to ask for what they desire and stop discussing and fighting over the methods which they think will bring about the desired end," said Mr. Hooke.

"In a Social Credit state," said the speaker, "as a true democracy, the individual is supreme, and the state is a contrivance through which the collection of individuals are able to gain their desired ends. Governments are owned by the people and not the people by governments," he said.

The new session of the house, said Mr. Duke in seconding the throne speech reply, "is the first of a series that will make history not only in the province of Alberta, but in the whole of Canada at least—if not in the world.

"This government," he asserted, "has carefully laid the foundation. We are now ready to take active steps to implement the definitely-expressed will of the people at the last election in August, 1935. More and more are joining the ranks of those who say that the present financial system is antiquated and cannot function in an age of plenty," claimed the Rocky Mountain member.

"The people with true democratic spirit are declaring that which is evident to everyone—that there is a great lack of purchasing power in the hands of the consumers—and with one voice they are demanding that the money monopolists, those who are responsible for the supply of purchasing power, must remedy this deficiency.

"These money monopolists claim to be experts. They should be able to design a scheme, therefore, to give the people what they demand. I, for one, claim that it is the duty of this assembly so to legislate that the will of the people will be granted."

Mr. Duke, from his bench at the back of the house, declared that "this government has moved with great care and caution; they have studied the situation from every angle; they have compiled statistics which reveal definitely the conditions prevailing in Alberta; with great care they have secured the advice of technical experts who, in collaboration with Major Douglas, have given the Social Credit board, and through it the government, directions concerning the procedure by which the people in association will be able to secure that which is necessary, and which they demand as their right.

"It is now our duty to give these directions legislative authority. And I, for one, do not wish to have any delay in so doing."

The whole world, declared Mr. Duke, is watching the Alberta experiment and "many people are hoping that we may succeed." Because of that, he said, "no institution or no minority group of this province should attempt to put anything in the way of our endeavors to solve the present unsatisfactory conditions prevalent in this province, and in fact in the world."

He hoped, he said, that even the members of the official opposition in the legislature would remain silent if they could not endorse the steps to be taken, and thereby evade the discredit that will fall upon them and their party through any such opposition. "The people of this province are all determined, and will not look with favor upon any attempt to prevent the solution of their difficulties, for political purposes or any other reasons."

Mr. Duke said that 750,000 people "have the right by majority vote to decide for themselves what system shall prevail within the realm of their own boundaries." He would not suppose, he said, "that any outside body—business, financial or political—would presume to try to interfere with such a large body of people who are peacefully and definitely trying to solve their own troubles."

He concluded: "If democracy means anything at all, and if civilization is of any value to mankind, surely the British ideal of government must prevail. And I, as a loyal Britisher, will stand to the last on this ground."

8 ONE ASTOUNDING BILL BEFORE HOUSE

Edmonton Journal
August 4, 1937

The bill to amend the Alberta Social Credit act, which was introduced yesterday, is not only unprecedented in Alberta history but in that of any part of the world which possesses democratic institutions. It is expected to be followed by at least one other piece of legislation that also will be of a drastic character. So there can be no doubt any longer that, as forecast, the session will have wide repercussions.

The central feature of the measure that was presented after the very brief debate on the speech from the throne was concluded is the greatly increased authority it gives to the Social Credit board. To the powers conferred on that body when the act was passed in April this is added:

> To consider and if it is thought advisable to adopt proposals for making available the credit of the people of the province and to transmit to the commis-

sion any proposals so adopted and to give direction to the commission for the carrying out of the same.

Thus the board is empowered, without any restrictions upon it being imposed, to put into force any system it sees fit so long as this carried the name of Social Credit. It may turn everything in the province upside down in attempting to give effect to the theories of the advisers by whom it is being guided.

The house, if it passes the bill, will be conferring blanket legislative authority upon five of its private members whose experience is of the most limited character and who have not shown qualities that would justify the entrusting to them of any large responsibility.

It is hard to believe that the elected representatives of the people of the province would even consider the surrender to this extent of the functions they were chosen to discharge.

With such a proposal before the house, and others that may be as farreaching still to come, there can be no excuse whatever for the hurrying through of the session in a few days, as has been suggested. The least that is to be looked for is that legislation of this kind will be discussed thoroughly before it is placed on the statute books.

If that is done, it is surely not too much to hope that the rank and file of the members, bearing in mind their responsibility for the present and future welfare of the province, will refuse to sanction what is provided for by the bill that is now before them or by any others that may have been drafted along similar lines.

---

9 TRUE DEMOCRACY DAWNS IN ALBERTA?

Today & Tomorrow
August 5, 1937

Suave, debonaire Solon E. Low, Provincial Treasurer in the world's first Social Credit government, stood in the Legislative Chamber Wednesday, and in less than two dozen quiet words changed the destiny of eight hundred thousand citizens of Alberta.

It was an epic moment, intense climax to the provincial drama of the past few weeks, and the youthful minister was quite worthy of it.

Handling his pregnant charge with statesmanlike dignity and aplomb, Mr. Low begged leave to introduce his "Bill: an Act to Provide for the Regulation of the Monetization of the Credit of Alberta," before a House electric with anticipation and almost prostrate with suspense. [His words] ...were ...so momentous that within seconds they were flashing across the world. Thunderous applause broke from government benches; galleries were a hub-bub of whispered comments; page boys were darting swallows; pressmen scrambling Mercurys, shooting inky bullets through the machine-gun telegraph machines.

Mr. Low announced abolition of the Sales Tax—"something which, under pressure from Finance, this government itself imposed." This, he claimed, was a dividend; "for a tax is a dividend in reverse." And the House buzzed again.

Thus, on August 4, 1937, twenty-three years after Britain entered the suicidal economic war of 1914, a commoner declared war in Alberta's name, on the vested interests which alone make suicidal war possible. Near him sat William Aberhart, the Albertan whose insistent call for positive action was answered by thousands of his countrymen. Above, in the Speaker's Gallery, were G.F. Powell and L.D. Byrne, trusted associates of Major C.H. Douglas, technical advisers to Alberta, heralds of the New Democracy. Below, G.L. MacLachlan, whose mission brought them here.

The introduction came unexpectedly, injecting swift drama into a drama-packed afternoon. Time and again outsiders had expected the bill, only to be disappointed. Still they were intrigued by the swift comings and goings of the ministers. More than one henchman of finance was there, fretting at the delay, the atmosphere of mystery that permeated the chamber.

And the weak opposition, pitifully striving to serve the rusty god of outmoded party politics, fretted with them as they probed ...probed. And found nothing.

It was ironic that they, who so earnestly yearned for details of the new legislation, were privileged to demand hold-over of any clause in any lesser bill. And they could hardly refuse. There were quibbles, clashes; quips from the agile tongue of Mr. Duggan, barbed shafts from the irrepressible Unwin. But no main bill.

Recess and deadline for the daily papers. Then, business again, and now the Premier rose, hesitating a little over his words. The House tensed. Was this it? Silence blanketed the chamber.

The Premier continued: " ...an act to amend the School Assessment Act."

Laughter broke out everywhere. It was a neat stroke, beautifully timed. And everyone there appreciated it.

Suddenly, quietly, the Provincial Treasurer was on his feet. As is his wont, he had perfect command of himself.

"I beg leave to introduce a Bill ..."

The big news broke. Mr. Low spoke for some time. "The Bill," begged Mr. Duggan. "When do we get the Bill?"

"Immediately."

"Tonight?"

"Immediately."

Immediately was an eternity for the stalwarts of the old-line parties. Perhaps, in the printed sheets they received a few seconds later, they read the death warrant of their own senile creed. And the birth certificate of a cleaner, deeper, more humane philosophy.

Just what does the new enactment mean? It means that every banker doing business within the province must apply for and obtain a license from a Provincial Credit Commission to be appointed. It means that every bank employee must also apply for and obtain a license. It means that the Provincial Credit Commission has the power to cancel any license of any licensee who commits a breach of certain undertakings mentioned in the act. It means that if the banks will not cooperate with Alberta in her endeavors to banish insecurity, then Alberta ...will not cooperate with them!

Together with sister legislation introduced since the opening of the Special Session on August 3, the Monetization Act provides a battering ram capable of shattering any barricades the finance powers may erect. No matter where a bank operates, it will be under the watchful eye of The People; for Local Directorates—appointed by banker and social credit board—will 'ride herd' on the money institutions constantly.

Stiff penalties are provided for violation of the act. No interference with any person in the province will be brooked.

Alberta means business!

---

10 BANK CONTROL BILL

Edmonton Journal
August 5, 1937

Of the bill that is designed to give control of the banks in Alberta to the Social Credit board there is really only one thing that needs to be said. This is that beyond question the proposed legislation goes beyond the constitutional powers of the province.

Among the "classes of subjects" placed by the B.N.A. act within the exclusive authority of the parliament at Ottawa is that defined as: "Banking, incorporation of banks and the issue of paper money." In the exercise of that authority parliament has passed the Bank act, under which alone banks can carry on operations legally. If the province should try to control these institutions in accordance with the terms of the bill that was introduced in the legislature yesterday, it would be violating the law under which the dominion came into existence. It cannot do so without the most serious consequences to Alberta.

Mr. Aberhart states that the legislation will "in no way rob the banks of anything whatever nor can it possibly interfere with the way in which they order their business." But it does undertake to put each branch under five directors, three to be appointed by the Social Credit board and two by the "Banker." They are to "supervise, direct and control the policy of the Banker." Yet the premier says that the proposed act cannot possibly interfere with the way in which the banks order their business. Could anything be more absurd than such a claim in the face of what is provided for in the bill?

At the moment it is unnecessary to consider other features of this extraordinary measure—the licensing of the institutions themselves and of their employees, the penalties that are imposed and much else. Nor is any purpose to be served by seeking to elucidate the meaning of the Douglas phraseology that is incorporated in the preamble and that serves thus as a basis for what follows.

There is, however, one clause that has a humorous aspect. "No provision of this act," it reads, "shall be construed as to authorize the doing of any act or thing which is not within the legislative competence of the legislative assembly." This comes after the bill has provided for the doing of all sorts of acts and things that quite obviously the legislature has no legal right to authorize.

There is no doubt how the courts would construe these provisions. But on the same day another bill was put before the legislature which seeks to prevent the courts from hearing any action "concerning the constitutional validity of any enactment of the legislative assembly" without the government's permission. So the government is not only setting out to do what is expressly forbidden to the province by the B.N.A. act but to bar citizens from securing judicial redress for any wrong they may have suffered through the legislature's disregard of the law of the land.

11 SHAKING THE WORLD

Calgary Herald
August 6, 1937

Warned in advance by their own legal advisers that no court will ever accept it as law, the Aberhart government are railroading through a make-believe bank-licensing bill. Just as the Kaiser of Doorn still posed as Emperor with only a wood-pile for his empire, so these Edmonton crusaders are solemnly passing bogus legislation with the boast that they are implementing "the people's will."

The Attorney-General was honest enough to tell the House yesterday that he had given the government his opinion on these bills. Hon. Mr. Low had chosen to remain insolently "dumb" (the word is his own) as to the nature of that opinion; Mr. Hugill made a chivalrous effort not to let his colleague down. But his cautious responses left it plain as day that the bills had, in advance, been pronounced unconstitutional.

It will not be surprising if, for this crime of honesty, Mr. Hugill is presently deprived of his portfolio. In point of fact, however, he did less to reveal the truth of the situation than Mr. Low had already done. A politician does not remain dumb when he can score a point;

and if Mr. Low had been able to say that the government's scheme was approved by its legal department he would have said so. His silence was the most eloquent performance he has ever given on the floor of the Legislature.

And thus Alberta knows that, instead of reform, its "social credit" government is today forcing through another dead-letter law, with full knowledge that it is a dead-letter before it is even signed.

Such is the fulfilment of the "social credit" program organized by the Douglas experts, such the momentous climax that was to "shake the world."

It may well shake the world—with laughter.

12 BACK TO THE MIDDLE AGES!

Edmonton Journal
August 6, 1937

How far the Aberhart government is prepared to go in applying its Social Credit theories and in penalizing those who do not agree with it is illustrated by three bills presently before the house. Each of these restricts the right of appeal to the courts or paves the way for other invasion of civil rights.

Under one bill no person will be allowed to ask the courts to decide whether any Alberta law is contrary to the fundamental law of Canada—unless the government first grants permission for such an action. If an Alberta law is within the powers of the province, there is no need to fear an appeal to the courts; if it is beyond provincial powers, then no citizen of Canada should be deprived of his right under the Canadian constitution to seek the protection of the courts against it.

Another opens with the following paragraph which sets forth the purpose of the legislation:

An act to provide for the restriction of the civil rights of certain persons.

At least, that is frank and aboveboard! In this act, the Social Credit government seeks again by legislative enactment to destroy a fundamental right of every Canadian citizen. The act states that a specified group of citizens of Alberta, many in humble circumstances, under certain conditions shall not be "capable of bringing, maintaining or defending"—mark that word "defending"—"any action in any court of civil jurisdiction in the province which has for its object the enforcement of any claim either in law or equity."

The third bill, amending the "Alberta Social Credit act," paves the way for further restrictions of civil rights. Under it, any person in Alberta may find himself deprived of the right of appealing to or defending himself in the courts of justice. Any farmer, any merchant, any worker, may not only be denied this right, but may have restricted or denied to him other liberties, enjoyed by other Canadian citizens if the Social Credit board should deem that such action were desirable for the purpose of "promoting, conserving or enhancing the social credit of the province," and the lieutenant-governor-in-council should concur in that opinion.

Right of appeal to the courts is a civil right cherished deeply by every Canadian. It is a right enshrined in British tradition, won only after a long period of struggle. It is a right that has been upheld in the dominion, that has been accepted as fundamental in all parts of the empire. Even the lowest pariah in India is not denied access to the courts.

It is time for the people of Alberta to make their voices heard definitely and unmistakably in protest against this threatened gross and far-reaching infringement of civil rights within the province.

If Social Credit cannot be made effective in Alberta without the withdrawal of fundamental civil rights, then its inauguration means the ushering in of a reign of terror, a return to the unsafe, autocratic conditions of the middle ages. THE JOURNAL cannot bring itself to believe that any substantial number of people want Social Credit at any such price.

13 OUSTING OF MR. HUGILL

Edmonton Journal
August 7, 1937

The demand for Mr. Hugill's resignation became inevitable after his statement in the legislature on Thursday. When asked as to whether it was within the powers of the house to pass the bill it was discussing then, the attorney-general replied that "acts on banking and banks are assigned under Section 91 to the parliament of Canada and therefore we have not the right."

By expressing his honest opinion, the correctness of which is not open to doubt, Mr. Hugill made it impossible for him to continue in his post. The government was determined on having legislation enacted that was clearly in defiance of the constitution of the country. Having set out on that course, it was bound to dispense with the services of its chief law officer who preferred not to be "dumb"—to use the term the provincial treasurer applied to himself on information from him being sought in regard to the legal advice the ministers had received—but to answer frankly when questioned respecting the province's powers.

Mr. Hugill is the fourth minister to leave the cabinet within a few months. Three of them have been dismissed and one has resigned voluntarily. He was the last of the original "right" or moderate wing of the government to retain his portfolio and the wonder is that his retirement has been delayed so long.

Those best able to judge are agreed that Mr. Hugill has done excellent work in the administration of his department. He has shown a high sense of his duty, though it is obvious how serious were the difficulties in the discharge of this that he encountered, through the policies which the government as a whole wished to put into effect. The very circumstances under which he has surrendered his post constitute a tribute to his integrity.

14 SOCIAL CREDIT AND BANKING

Edmonton Bulletin
August 9, 1937

Declaring that the provincial government of which he is the leader has no intention of interfering with the regular business of banking, Premier William Aberhart, in addressing the Edmonton Prophetic Bible Conference at the Strand theatre on Sunday evening as part of a Social Credit rally of the various Edmonton zones of the organization, stated that the government did desire "an investigation into the usurped right of monetizing our credit and holding a monopoly in that regard that is detrimental to the welfare of our citizens."

Highlight of the evening's proceedings came when Premier Aberhart read to the large audience a cablegram received from Major Douglas in London in which the founder of Social Credit applauded the action of the government in its legislation affecting banks, their operation and their staffs.

The cablegram read "Good work. Rush appointment of bank directors."

The message was one of a number received from scattered parts of the province assuring the government of their support in the furtherance of policies initiated at the recent special session of the legislature.

The premier was the main speaker at the rally which was one of the most largely attended in the history of Social Credit in this city.

The Strand theatre was filled to the limit of its capacity of more than 1,200 while an overflow audience was accommodated at the Empress theatre, where an additional 800 were taken care of and listened to the proceedings at the Strand by way of the loud speaker system.

The rally was held as a general enthusiasm for the movement throughout the various city zones and groups of the Social Credit organization and was a prelude to a larger and more comprehensive rally to be held two weeks hence to commemorate the second anniversary of the general election at which the Social Credit forces were returned to power.

The program of the rally was large and comprehensive. It opened with a hymn, Sir Arthur Sullivan's immortal "Onward Christian Soldiers." The rally call was given after each stanza. Then there followed the Invocation. A tenor solo, "The Great Adventure" was sung by George Turner.

Then there followed a scene in which all members of the Edmonton Council of Strategy appeared on the stage and took part in a round table discussion.

Then came violin solo. Ethelbert Nevin's "The Rosary" played by Richard Seaborn. The offering and announcements followed, after which came the reading of telegrams and acknowledgments of support. Following this came a few words of advice on "How to Read the Bible." Mr. Williams then sang, "I Heard the Voice of Jesus Say."

Short speeches of greeting were then given by the zone presidents and this was followed by the theme song and the Benediction.

Dealing with the economic situation confronting the province and the government, the premier said that "Our task is of a twofold nature.

"First we have the conceivement of the solution which in itself, you must know is magnitudinal. Second there is the greater task of enlightening the people along lines which will displace ignorance and delusion with knowledge and definite truth.

"Last week in Calgary I tried to point out to the people something of the enormity and vast extent of our potential natural resources. I merely gave quotations from some of the reports filed in our offices. But what a hubbub it caused among the old line parties. Enlightenment of the people is an element which is a most disturbing factor and it causes much uneasiness in the minds of the opposing forces. These forces know that only by keeping the people in ignorance are they enabled to retain them in economic slavery.

"These forces find great consolation in the much worn words 'constitutionality' and 'ultra vires'. They use these words most freely with the hope that it may have the desired effect of striking awe in the minds of the people and leaving the sanctum sanctorum of finance untrespassed and unmolested. The very air screams with these awful words today, especially since our last session.

"May I assure our people that we have no intention of interfering with the regular business of banking, but we do desire an investigation into the usurped right of monetizing our credit and holding a monopoly in that regard that is detrimental to the welfare of our citizens.

"Surely the banking institutions can not claim to be above and beyond all direction and control in connection with the provincial law and civil right. If so, something is desperately wrong.

"If they declare our acts unconstitutional or if they disallow them in the face of the strongly expressed will of the people to the contrary, surely the welfare of our people is not being considered by those who would thus act.

"They are saying how do we know the people are behind you. The only way this can be ascertained is by the prompt and general declaration of that fact in the papers and over the radio and in every way possible. Democracy must declare itself."

The premier announced that during the present week he and Hon. Lucien Maynard, minister of municipal affiars, will make a tour through the Battle River and St. Paul districts, speaking at the following points: Wednesday afternoon, Ashmont; Wednesday night, St. Paul; Thursday afternoon, Battle River and Thursday night at Lac la Biche. Friday meetings have not yet been arranged.

A vote was taken of the people in the Strand and Empress theatres as to whether they favored the principles of true democracy as enunciated in the Social Credit program. Both audiences voted overwhelmingly in favor of these principles.

"Evidently the people of Edmonton and district are ready to make themselves heard if any one seeks to thwart what they know they have a right to demand," declared Premier Aberhart in making known results of the votes. "It thrills us to hear them vote so enthusiastically," he said.

The premier then said that "Someone has said that Social Credit is a great adventure. We do not mean by that that there is no reality to it, but that it is the discovery of new relationships, new methods and new delights.

"It calls for bravery and courage. It demands unity in association.

"When we have travelled the way, others will follow with greater ease.

It necessitates a spirit of enterprise, a persistent determination of endurance and a love for freedom, justice and our fellows."

The premier then described for the radio audience the scene in the Strand theatre. He described how they were seated on the platform, in horseshoe fashion. Hon. E.C. Manning, minister of trade and industry and provincial secretary; Hon. D.B. Mullen, minister of agriculture; N.B. James, M.L.A. for Acadia, who has spoken frequently over the Bible Conference meetings in the last several months, the six presidents or their representatives of the various zones covering the whole Edmonton north and south areas.

Behind and on either side of these were the presidents of the various 40 groups of Edmon-

ton "who can bring us the viewpoint of the citizens of the city and district" said the premier.

Seated at the piano was Mrs. E.C. Manning "our genial and popular accompanist," and near her were the assisting artists of the night, Messrs. Turner, Williams and Seaborn.

"Before me," said the premier, "the theatre is packed, not only in the boxes but right up in the gallery. We have met here on a very auspicious occasion. The legislature has just closed its session at which you know, some very important steps were taken in connection with the introduction of Social Credit.

This great audience both here and in the Empress theatre, would indicate to everyone that the people of this province are determined to see some attempt made to solve their difficulties. We fully appreciate this support tonight and thank all these presidents and representatives for helping us on the platform."

Hon. Mr. Mullen then said that as this was a meeting of the council of strategy it might be of interest to show the public the workings of such meeting. He then asked Orvis A. Kennedy to explain why this meeting was being held in public.

Mr. Kennedy said that "We are broadcasting our deliberations of tonight's council because this is in accordance with the two great principles of a true democracy. We recognize that the first great principle of a true democracy is that the people have an inherent right, with full information to hand, to declare publicly and definitely, what they want and what they expect to get under the circumstances.

"The second great principle of a true democracy is that the people must audibly and visibly, express their pleasure and approval when their representatives accomplish what the people want and they will vociferously voice their objection and disapproval to those who try to prevent the same."

The council next turned its attention to a discussion of whether a change was needed in the financial system.

Premier Aberhart declared that "The most evident reason is that the present system fails to distribute our products efficiently. This causes a glut on the market and unemployment immediately follows."

Hon. Mr. Mullen declared that, "If we expect to distribute more, we must have more goods to distribute. There is nothing to be gained by sharing up what we now have. The real problem for our experts is to bring our man and machine power which is for the most part standing idly by into grips with our great natural resources. Surely this can be done."

Premier Aberhart: "It surely can. But in the meantime the people must maintain their unity of purpose and their determination. They must secure the cooperation of all their neighbors and friends. They must all be agreed to ask for increased purchasing power by way of monthly dividends and they must demand a lower cost to live."

Hon. Mr. Manning: "This is our suggestion. To bring the matter to the attention of every citizen and to give them a chance to declare themselves, we have prepared a true blue unity of purpose ballot.

"These should be signed by every citizen who desires increased purchasing power by way of monthly dividends and a lower cost to live. Each person should try to get his friends and neighbors to sign the true blue ballot."

As a concluding feature, the six zone presidents were introduced and each spoke briefly.

---

15 RUNNING WILD

Calgary Herald
August 12, 1937

OTTAWA, Aug. 12—A decision by the Alberta government on Prime Minister Mackenzie King's plan for a court test on constitutionality of the province's bank-license legislation, will be delayed at least until Monday, it was indicated here today.

Prime Minister King made public a telegram from Provincial Secretary E.C. Manning which said "Premier (Aberhart) and several ministers absent until Monday. Your wire will be brought to premier's attention immediately upon his return."

At Bonnyville, Alta., last night, Premier Aberhart said he would call a special meeting of the Alberta cabinet but did not indicate when.

In a telegram to Premier Aberhart yesterday, Mr. King suggested a co-operative appeal to the Supreme Court to test the legislative competence of Alberta to pass three statutes. They were the act requiring bankers to take out licenses and subscribe to control by the provincial government.

OTTAWA, Aug. 12—Mr. Mackenzie King's telegram to Premier Aberhart last night is construed to confirm beyond a doubt, the intention of the Dominion government to refer to the Supreme Court the legislative acts of last week's special session of the Alberta legislature. There has been no reference yet, but when Mr. King says the minister of justice is "considering" it, he really means that the government is doing just that. They have been doing it several days. The course now so plainly indicated is the course thought most likely to be followed.

The telegram to Mr. Aberhart was based on two considerations—the gravest doubts, entertained by legal authorities here and apparently everywhere else, as to the constitutional validity of the enactments and the hope that Mr. Aberhart does not wish to do anything illegal. There is a further consideration—a great deal is heard about provincial rights. Such a thing as federal rights are also to be mentioned. In this case the provincial government is held to encroach on what are regarded as the unassailable rights of the Dominion.

When this is attempted, the opinion of many here is that the government cannot sit idly by and "take it". If it were inclined to take that position, it would be dislodged from it by the claims, amounting almost to clamor, that what Mr. Aberhart proposes may undermine the whole banking and credit structure of the country. A common view is that the government at Edmonton, so to speak, is "running wild" and that it is time the check were applied.

The right of the government to refer to the court a provincial statute is as clear as it is to refer a federal statute or abstract question of law.

The consent of Premier Aberhart to the process is considered desirable and also his undertaking to suspend the operation of his Acts. But, if he refuses to do either, it does not in any way impede the right of the Dominion government to go ahead on its own initiative.

If Mr. Aberhart should decline to appoint counsel to argue his side of the case, the Dominion government can do it for him and doubtless it would. Any interested party, pro or con, can also be represented.

The projected process of referring the matter to the courts is a precaution lest, by some chance, it might be held that the statutes come within the legislative competence of the province.

Though the Dominion government has the power of disallowance, no wish to exercise it peremptorily is displayed. The government prefers the intermediary course of a reference to the courts. If the tribunal hold the legislation is bad, no doubt disallowance would follow. If conceivably, it should hold it to be intra vires of the legislature, the right to disallow would still prevail though its exercise would be more questionable.

As Mr. Aberhart is up north, the immediate answer requested last evening took the form only of an acknowledgement. So instead of today it probably will be next week before formal action is taken.

The supreme court meets on Oct. 5, and any government reference is given precedence. Meanwhile, matters will be facilitated if the Aberhart government takes steps to defend its enactment, and consents to stay the enforcement of statutes whose validity are subject to such a grave constitutional doubt.

If Mr. Aberhart won't "play ball", as it were, and will not agree to a court reference or suspension of the enactments, the government may very well decide to disallow them, peremptorily, without further ado. It has the power to do so. The minister of justice casually remarked last evening that a "mess might be created" if enforcement of the acts is attempted while their judicial determination is being sought by the government here.

Following is message sent by Prime Minister King to Premier Aberhart last evening:

"Minister of justice is considering under provisions British North America Act certain legislation enacted at recent session of Alberta legislature. Before submitting the question for decision of governor-in-council would appreciate your letting me know whether your government would be willing to facilitate hearing of a reference to the Supreme Court of Canada regarding the validity of bills numbers five, six and nine and to undertake, pending determination of such reference not to take any steps towards enforcement of any of said measures.

"The reference would be made under section fifty-five of the Supreme Court Act which provides for reference by the governor-in-counsel [sic] of important questions of law or fact touching the powers of the provincial legislatures. In view of urgency of matter would appreciate immediate reply."

16 DOMINION CABINET RULING

Calgary Herald
August 12, 1937

OTTAWA, Aug. 12—The Dominion government announced early this evening the Alberta bank legislation, passed at the recent session of the provincial legislature, has been disallowed.

Action was taken on recommendation of Hon. Ernest Lapointe minister of justice, who declared the legislature of Alberta "deliberately attempts to interfere with the operation of Dominion laws and to substitute laws and institutions of its own for those legitimately enacted and organized by parliament."

The three Alberta statutes disallowed are:

1. An act to license banks.

2. An act to license bank employees.

3. An act to close the courts to any application seeking invalidation of Alberta legislation.

Following a meeting of cabinet council late today Prime Minister Mackenzie King revealed that the recommendation for disallowance had been before cabinet last Wednesday but action had been delayed while he discussed with Premier Aberhart of Alberta the suggestion that the acts be referred to the Supreme Court of Canada.

Today the government had before it Mr. Aberhart's reply which was a refusal. Notice of disallowance will be forwarded to the Lieutenant-Governor of Alberta, and also published in a special edition of the Canada Gazette. Disallowance is effective immediately.

DON QUIXOTE RIDES AGAIN

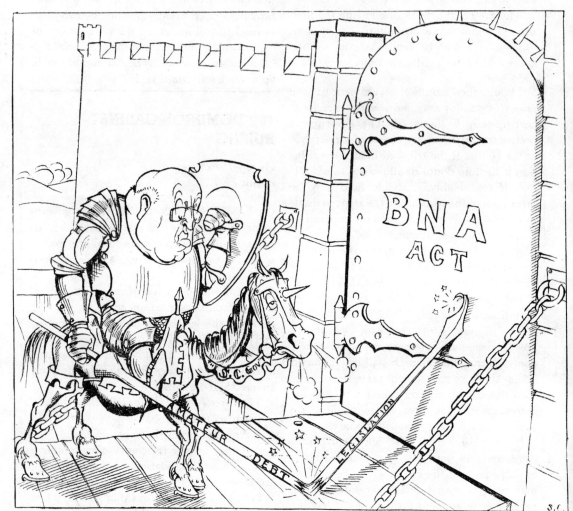

From Stewart Cameron, No Matter How Thin You Slice It.
By permission of Mrs. Thelma Cameron.

Premier Aberhart's tilts at the "money barons" were later to develop into legislation designed to cripple the financial institutions of the province and gave grave concern to thousands of small investors throughout Canada who had put their faith and cash in Alberta's investments. But the British North America Act proved a bulwark against amateur debt legislation. Court after court declared government debt legislation invalid or unconstitutional with the result that "Don Quixote" Aberhart ceased to tilt at windmills and turned his blunted lance against the Federal constitution with the results pictured above.   (February 27, 1937.)

PUNISHED BUT NOT PENITENT

From Stewart Cameron, No Matter How Thin You Slice It.
By permission of Mrs. Thelma Cameron.

Refusing to be party to legislation which he knew was not within powers of the provincial legislature, Attorney-General John W. Hugill, of Calgary, resigned his office. On September 23 he renounced his pledges to the government and stated he would go into opposition. The Premier's punishment of his former cabinet colleague had failed to silence him.   (September 25, 1937.)

17 PREMIER DUMFOUNDED

Edmonton Journal
August 16, 1937

CALGARY, Aug. 16—Telegram from Prime Minister King suggesting that the Alberta government agree to a reference to the supreme court of Canada on validity of the bank licensing legislation passed at the last session of the legislature "dumbfounded" Premier Aberhart, the latter declared during the Prophetic Bible institute service in Calgary Sunday.

"When I received the telegram, I need not say to you that I was dumbfounded to think such a request should come from the prime minister of Canada," Premier Aberhart said.

"I did not expect the federal government to take up the cause of the money interests," he continued. "We are prepared to meet the money interests but we did not expect to have to meet the federal government as well."

Banks which refused to function as the government asked them to do, while claiming the privileges of their charters, were no different from individuals who took relief and refused to work, said the premier.

"Let the banks fight their own battles, not leave them to the federal government," he said. "I am sure the federal government will be willing to back up the will of the people of Alberta. The banks will then begin to serve the people. Everything will then be lovely—let's hope that's true. But if it's not true the voice of 800,000 people can be heard pretty plainly!

"We are a part of Canada. We have no desire to separate from the other parts. No matter how radical our policies may seem we want it known that we are loyal to our king, to our God and to our country."

Premier Aberhart declared it would have been more in keeping with "good statesmanship" if the prime minister of Canada or the governor-general-in-council had put into action a policy of "Hands off Alberta" and support the Alberta government.

He continued:

"The telegram came when I was away in the far north and east of our province, looking over conditions to see how they could be improved. I had only a few hours in Edmonton on my return before taking the train for Calgary. I took the telegram with me down here and have studied it since I left Edmonton. In addition to this, many of our ministers are very busy at the present time covering the province to investigate conditions that must be improved, if possible, in the near future.

"You can quite understand that ministers cannot stay behind their desks all the time. We are holding a council meeting Monday, and if possible, we shall make reply by Monday afternoon or Monday evening. We cannot do better than that. It must be considered carefully. I need not say that the telegram came somewhat as a shock to us. We have no intention of interfering with the regular business of banking, or with the welfare of the people in the provinces to the east or west of us. We are simply trying to solve our own problems. We are not going to deal with the banks' monopoly of issuing currency. The province is given the control of its property and civil rights. We intend to hold these. No institution has any right to try to wrench these rights from the hands of our people.

"No financial institution has the right to deprive the people of their property and civil rights by usurping the power to maintain our credit. The shock of the telegram was all the greater when we remembered the public utterances of the present prime minister of Canada when he sought the support of our citizens. The phrase 'hands off Alberta', still rings in our ears, and the recent statement regarding maintenance of our credit—depriving us of the right of responsible people—has not been so quickly forgotten by us.

"It would appear to me that there must be some misunderstanding somewhere, or the telegram would never have been sent. It seems to me that we must present our case most carefully, so that all concerned may understand all about it, and then, when they act, it will be with full knowledge of the people. Probably the unanimity of opinion that has been expressed, and the definite mandate that the Alberta government has been given by our people is not known to them away down east. I note by the papers that some of you collectively have been informing them in no uncertain terms, but time will reveal the whole story.

"You may count on your government giving this telegram our most careful and courteous consideration. The will of the people, however, should be definitely recognized by all in the face of the proper interpretation of our constitution. It will be most difficult for all our people to understand that which forces the citizens to continue to suffer hardship and privation. Christ, himself, would say on occasions of this kind: "The constitution was made for the people—not the people for the constitution."

18 ACT IS INVASION OF FEDERAL FIELD

Edmonton Bulletin
August 18, 1937

OTTAWA, Aug. 18—The Alberta statute to force bankers to take our licenses and subscribe to provincial control is "an unmistakable invasion" of the legislative field of the Dominion parliament. Justice Minister Ernest Lapointe laid down that opinion yesterday when recommending to the Federal government disallowance of the statute and two others concerning access to the courts. His recommendation was adopted and the three laws vetoed.

The acts, the minister of justice found, "conflict with Dominion laws and virtually supplant Dominion institutions designed by parliament to facilitate the trade and commerce of the whole Dominion."

Operation of the Alberta laws would lead to "confusion and injury to the public interest of Canada."

The minister of justice, in concluding his review of the legislation, laid down this general opinion of the power of the disallowance.

"While the undersigned is of the opinion that no project of policy of a provincial legislature should be interfered with by exercise of the power of disallowance merely on the ground that measures to promote such project or policy are of doubtful constitutional validity, a distinction is to be made where the legislature deliberately attempts to interfere with the operation of Dominion laws and to substitute laws and institutions of its own for those legitimately enacted and organized by parliament and this is particularly true where the legislature has denied recourse to the courts of justice."

19 SOCRED TO FIGHT OTTAWA EDICT

Edmonton Bulletin
August 18, 1937

Alberta will fight along constitutional lines in its battle to enforce recent bank legislation, Premier Aberhart stated Tuesday at a social credit picnic at Lakeview Beach on South Cooking lake.

When told at the meeting that the Dominion government had disallowed three acts passed at a recent session of the provincial Legislature, the Premier announced the Dominion government's action to the crowd a few minutes later.

"You see what you are up against," he added.

"Give us a gun," a man shouted. Other members of the crowd of about 350 persons were silent.

"No. No—None of that," Premier Aberhart replied quickly.

"This is not bloodshed," he continued. "It is constitutional. We'll stand by the constitution and fight it through. May I suggest to you that you never allow anybody to tell you we are going to secede from our great Dominion. We have no desire to leave the home of our forefathers.

"We may disagree with their prejudices but we'll stand together and fight together, and try to solve our difficulties. We want to be allowed to fight out our differences in our own real home.

"As members of a great Dominion, will you keep steady and go ahead on lines we have always stood for?"

Without a full report on the Dominion government's action, Premier Aberhart had no comment to make to reporters. The Alberta cabinet was scheduled to meet and it was believed disallowance of the Alberta legislation would be discussed then.

Provincial Secretary E.C. Manning, who charged banks manipulated the amount of interest available in Canada for their own gain, and Floyd M. Baker, member of the legislature for Clover Bar and secretary of the Social Credit Board, were the other speakers. The picnic was sponsored by the Clover Bar Social Credit Association.

"It is a constitutional fight and we'll carry

on," the premier continued in his address, "and the results will follow for I am persuaded the British constitution is the greatest constitution and I am satisfied there are some means in the British constitution for bringing to our people the food, clothing and shelter they need in this land of abundance.

"I believe we have in this province the greatest example of true democracy that the world has ever seen," the premier said. "By this I mean a government elected by the people and for the purpose of carrying out the will of the people."

The premier opened his address by telling the crowds that "we are in a real fight. Unless our hands are together we won't accomplish that which we hope to accomplish."

The suggestion from Prime Minister Mackenzie King that Alberta facilitate a reference to the Supreme Court of Canada of three acts passed recently by the Legislature was considered "very seriously" by the provincial government.

"We have tried to get into our hearts and minds what you would want us to do and what we considered the welfare of the province demands that we do," he added.

Mr. Aberhart said the government was determined "with all the force in us" to obtain for the people what they had demanded "if you keep asking for them." He listed as the demand from the people increased purchasing power, a lower cost of living and relief from taxation.

The people need not bother how these aims might be accomplished he stated, but could leave that to the experts chosen to do it.

"Don't let details bother you, ask for results," he declared.

"For goodness sake, don't get that inferiority complex," the premier continued. "You cannot get anything if you don't think you can get it. How? That is something you don't need to bother about. You go ahead with your farm work."

20 ABERHART CHALLENGES FEDERAL RIGHT OF DISALLOWANCE

Calgary Herald
August 20, 1937

Authority of the Dominion government to disallow provincial legislation was challenged in a telegram sent to Prime Minister Mackenzie King by Premier Aberhart in reply to notification from federal authorities that three Alberta acts had been disallowed.

Copies of the telegram were released here today by Premier Aberhart.

The Alberta reply "again asserts with all possible emphasis that the legislation in question is within the sphere of our jurisdiction" and charged disallowance of the banking legislation is "deliberately violating property and civil rights."

"Further disclosure of the institutions so self evidently inciting you to disallow our legislation will simultaneously saddle your government with full responsibility for producing a most serious constitutional crisis," Premier Aberhart's message warned.

The telegram, sent last night several hours after Premier Aberhart announced a special session of the legislature would be called to pass legislation substituting for that disallowed by the federal government, declared "OUR PEOPLE insist we are pledged to go forward in obedience to them, not to you nor to the banks."

'Frustrating us will not evade the final outcome and will only lead to OUR PEOPLE demanding with ever-increasing insistence that their will shall prevail," the wire added.

Challenging the right of the Dominion government to disallow any provincial legislation "because it has no such power today," Premier Aberhart's wire continued.

"This is the opinion of your own minister of justice who stated in parliament, March 30, 1937: 'I do not think in a federation such as this the power of disallowance could be exercised by the central government.'

"Then he went on to say: 'I believe the provincial legislatures would feel that they are still supreme and sovereign within the sphere of their jurisdiction.'

"We again assert with all possible emphasis that the legislation in question is within the sphere of our jurisdiction in which the clearly expressed will of OUR PEOPLE is supreme and sovereign."

Challenging the right of the Dominion "to invade a purely provincial field in delegating authority to any institution to control and restrict OUR PEOPLE'S credit," the wire charged such action was "deliberately violating property and civil rights. This constitutes social lawlessness which you should not support."

Asked whether the telegram meant the province would proceed with enforcement of the banking legislation despite disallowance, or whether some action was planned in the courts, the premier said he had "nothing to say at present about the next step."

No date has been set yet for the special session of the legislature, but the premier has announced it would be called as soon as possible after "negotiations" with the Dominion government have ended.

21   DISALLOWANCE DRAWS FIRE FROM C.C.F.

Edmonton Bulletin
August 23, 1937

A "glaring contrast" between the Dominion government's "swift and decisive action" in disallowing Alberta banking legislation and its "inaction" in regard to Quebec's so-called padlock law is noted in a statement released today by the national executive of the C.C.F.

"When it was a question of the civil liberties of the ordinary citizens of Quebec, the Dominion government promised to give 'serious consideration' to the proposal for a reference to the supreme court, and then did nothing; and it professed to believe that the power of disallowance had become obsolete" the statement over the signature of David Lewis, national secretary of the party said.

"But, when it is a matter of the civil liberties of bankers in Alberta, the Dominion government immediately proposed a reference to the supreme court, and, when that is rejected, promptly disallows not one, but three acts."

The C.C.F. executive charges "class discrimination" in the government action and quotes Hansard to show that on March 30, Hon. Ernest Lapointe, minister of justice, on

whose recommendation the Alberta acts were disallowed, assured the house of commons that the power of disallowance was obsolete.

"We are not," says the statement, "here pronouncing the merits or demerits of disallowance in either the Alberta or Quebec case. But every one of the reasons given for disallowing the Alberta acts applies with at least equal force to the Padlock act."

The statement also quotes a report of the Canadian Bar Association, presented at the annual meeting here last week which says Quebec legislation "takes away all the safeguards which even an ordinary criminal enjoys before conviction."

Alberta, the statement recalls, has had "previous experience of disallowance at the hands of Mr. Mackenzie King and Mr. Lapointe.

"Just 13 years ago, April 29, 1924, the Dominion disallowed an Alberta mineral taxation act, on petition of the Canadian Pacific Railway Company, the Hudson's Bay Company, the Western Land Company, the Calgary and Edmonton Land Company and others."

"It is difficult," the statement concludes, "to avoid the conclusion that the interests of bankers are closer to the government's heart than the democratic rights of Canadian citizens." It further demands "an immediate, full and candid explanation" of the government's reasons for reversing policy on disallowance.

22   MANDATE OF THE PEOPLE

Edmonton Journal
August 23, 1937

He will "obey the mandate of the people rather than the prime minister of Canada," Premier Aberhart told an audience of 800 people here Saturday night.

"You in the province of Alberta have been recognized by the world as the only true democracy that has ever existed," he assured the crowd.

"This government is determined to implement for you" the basic dividend that he had promised during the election campaign, the premier added.

The audience, largely French-Canadian,

jammed and overflowed the community hall, and the meeting was delayed an hour and 20 minutes while loud speaker equipment was brought from Edmonton to be set up outside.

Hon. Lucien Maynard, minister of municipal affairs, spoke in French. The rest of the meeting was in English, and speakers included Hon. D.B. Mullen, minister of agriculture, and Charles Holder, Social Credit member of the legislature for St. Albert constituency. Chairman was Horace Monpetit.

"Your government had absolutely decided to put these (bank) laws into effect," said Mr. Maynard.

(Sunday, Premier Aberhart delivered the sermon at the Moravian church at Bruderheim, 34 miles northeast of Edmonton. The crowd, which totalled 425, overflowed the church and some members of the congregation heard the service through a loud-speaker on the lawns outside. Although the day marked the second anniversary of the provincial election on which he rode to power, the premier made no mention of politics throughout the service. He preached on "The Unpardonable Sin." The church has been without a pastor for the past few months.)

Mr. Maynard told his Legal audience that the province was within its constitutional rights in the anti-banking and judicature legislation which the dominion disallowed.

"It is a great battle, for you and for us," he declared in French. "The bills which we passed were valid, absolutely legal. We are going to take control of the credit of the province of Alberta. We are going to do that. Don't think the battle is over."

He quoted Hon. Ernest Lapointe, federal minister of justice, as having said in the house of commons last February that a province should have control of property and civil rights according to the terms of the B.N.A. act. "And that included financial credit," said Mr. Maynard.

"Now he says they are ultra vires when we pass laws using those rights. Your government had absolutely decided to put these laws into effect.

"It is not the letter—it is the spirit of the constitution that is most important. The government must have the power to give the means of existence to laws which are the will of the people. The laws of God are more important than the laws of man."

He declared that he had been informed by a physician at St. Paul that a baby in that district had died of starvation some time ago. The doctor, he said, had been called to the home when the father was ill, and found the 15-month-old child dead of malnutrition.

"It is not the will of God that babies should die of starvation," he said. No constitution can stand against the divine laws. Your government has absolutely decided to put these laws into effect.

"We are not going to touch the other provinces. All we ask is to have the right to control our own province. We are going to take on the power necessary to permit the people of this province to live in a better way, and not on the border of misery and death.

"Is the dominion government going to exercise the power of veto? No!"

He referred to the constitutional issue in Manitoba in the 80's over Roman Catholic parochial schools and told his French-Canadian audience: "They would not allow it. They would not allow any advantage to the people of the province."

The will of the people "means everything," said Mr. Maynard, "the premier depends on you. Tell us to go on, and we will go on. Tell us to stop, and—very well. You must not be too critical. He is acting for the people entirely."

---

23 NEW PROTEST BY ABERHART

Edmonton Bulletin
August 27, 1937

Emphatic protest against both the personnel and terms of reference of the Royal Commission established by the Dominion government to investigate and report on the whole question of the taxation structure in this country has been forwarded to Rt. Hon. W.I. Mackenzie King, premier of Canada, by Premier William Aberhart.

The premier's wire declares that it is "entirely futile to make representations under present set-up."

The Royal Commission is headed by Chief Justice N.W. Rowell of the Ontario Supreme Court and includes Mr. Justice Thibadeau

Rinfret of the Quebec supreme court, John W. Dafoe of the Winnipeg Free Press, R.A. MacKay, professor of economics at the University of Dalhousie, and H.F. Angus, economics professor at the University of British Columbia.

The Premier also informs Premier King that he is forwarding a covering letter in which further detail is set forth. Full text of Premier Aberhart's wire is as follows:

> Rt. Hon. William Lyon
> Mackenzie King
> Prime Minister of Canada,
> Ottawa, Ontario.
> Alberta protests emphatically against both personnel and terms of reference of Royal Commission. Entirely futile to make representations under present set-up. Writing fully."

While no information has been given out by the government as to whether the entire personnel of the commission is protested, it is believed that there is a feeling that insufficient attention has been given to progressive western thought in the personnel; that there will be insufficient attention given to those matters that most concern the west, such as reduction of interest rates; reduction of debt generally and easing of taxation.

While protesting the personnel and terms of reference of the Royal Commission, it is learned that the province has not nominated any alternatives or additions to the commission.

It was also learned that if Premier King decides to add to the commission and invites a provincial nominee, that the government is prepared to submit a name for consideration.

Whether the protest launched on Friday by Premier Aberhart, which states that it is "futile" to make representations under the present set-up, means that the province will boycott the inquiry and submit no representations, is not yet known.

The covering letter to the wire is expected to be delivered to Premier King on Monday.

24 MORE LEGISLATION PLANNED

Edmonton Bulletin
August 30, 1937

The Dominion government would have more Alberta legislation "to disallow," Premier William Aberhart intimated when he addressed the Social Credit picnic at St. George's island Saturday afternoon commemorating the second anniversary of the party victory at the provincial polls.

The crowd was estimated by Social Credit officials at 20,000 persons.

Other speakers at the anniversary celebration were Hon. Lucien Maynard, minister of municipal affairs, who challenged the federal government with disallowing the Alberta bank legislation because it was afraid to test the legislation in the courts, and by Hon. E.C. Manning, provincial secretary, who emphasized the need for provincial control of credit.

A new session of the provincial legislature had been called because of the disallowance by Ottawa of the recent Alberta bank legislation, Premier Aberhart told the rally.

"If they've disallowed this act, I can assure you they'll have more to disallow," said the premier, "and I'm afraid they'll find it increasingly hard to disallow them."

"All that we're asking for is that the federal government shall monetize our credit as we desire—in comparison with our resources," he said. "We've got our hand on the lever and we're going ahead."

"It will show them how strong the movement here is when they hear that 20,000 people assembled here today for this meeting," he told the crowd.

The premier called for a "parliamentary vote" as to whether the people present at the rally wanted the government to proceed with its two objectives—a monthly dividend and a lower cost to live.

On the vote being called, the "Aye" came with a mighty roar, while not a single voice was raised when the premier asked for those opposed.

The premier also gave the crowd a fighting talk in support of the Alberta bank legislation. First he explained the legislation to the gathering.

"The Dominion government disallowed

our legislation because it was afraid to go to the courts with it," said Mr. Maynard. "Lapointe was afraid and the banks were afraid that the Privy Council would uphold the legality of it."

"We're not going to stop even if the Dominion government disallows our legislation," he said. "we're going to proceed—but within the law and within the constitution."

The speaker said that any law which contravened the law of God was "not constitutional."

Mr. Manning said that social credit had made such progress in Alberta as compared with the rest of the world because of the progressive attitude of the people of Alberta, the fact that the people of Alberta were the most enlightened on economic problems, and the fact that social credit was a practical issue.

Credit in the Dominion was contracted $766,000,000 between 1929 and 1937, he said, pointing out that the province must obtain control of the credit.

He warned that the people must not rely on the government alone to institute social credit, but must give full support.

"I look forward to the anniversary of the day the government takes over the complete control of credit. St. George's island won't be big enough to hold the crowd," concluded Mr. Manning.

The crowd adopted the suggestion of W.R. Herbert, chairman, to send a telegram to Prime Minister Mackenzie King, protesting disallowance of the Alberta bank legislation and indicating emphatic support of the provincial government.

25 M.L.A.s STUDY NEW BILLS AT EDMONTON

Albertan
September 27, 1937

Intention of action to defy the federal government on disallowed legislation, increased taxation on banks and consolidation of the licensing of trades and business act are being studied by members of the Alberta Legislature which resumes session Monday.

Constitutional questions arising from disallowance are expected to be debated when a resolution denying the right of the federal government to void provincial legislation is considered. The resultion [*sic*] also declares determination to implement the three disallowed acts.

The disallowed acts—licensing bankers, barring courts to unlicenced bank employees and preventing legal actions challenging the validity of Alberta statutes without government consent—are expected to be reintroduced during the special session.

Taxation of banks is estimated to bring the government around $1,000,000 in revenue annually. Notice of the tax bill has been given the legislature and the bill itself may be introduced Monday. It provides for increasing the tax on paid up capital and a new tax on reserves and undivided profits.

Consolidation of various licensing powers and amendments to certain powers is also before the legislature. The bill applies to "All trades, business, industries, employments and occupations ...except only any such business as is for the time being exempted from the operation of this act by order of the lieutenant-governor-in-council."

Several bills have yet to be introduced. One is expected to deal with the press but in what manner has not yet been disclosed.

26 AN EXTRAORDINARY BILL

Calgary Herald
September 28, 1937

That a thorough-going despotic sway is to be imposed on employers and employees in this province—with such exceptions as the government may decide—is indicated by the Licensing of Trades and Business Act introduced in the legislature.

It is not only extraordinary but highly sinister that any provincial government in this Dominion should attempt to go so far in the direction regimenting business activities and occupations of all kinds. It proposes to place in the hands of the youthful provincial secretary exceptional powers of discipline, to place under his individual control the fortunes of thousands of business men and highly qualified artisans, and to establish what may be easily converted into a very effective weapon for the disciplining of political opponents of the government. It provides no appeal against the dicta of one man who has never had any experience either in industry or business. The entire principle and purpose of the bill is objectionable.

Is one man to determine what businesses are to be carried on in this province? Is he to be empowered to tell one man he can carry on business and another that he is barred from doing so? A man who has carried on business honorably and successfully for many years can be prevented from doing so further by the minister of trade and industry. An experienced and capable artisan can be given similar summary treatment if Mr. Manning so decides.

The act is to apply to all trades, businesses, industries, employments and occupations in the province except those exempted by the cabinet. The minister of trade and industry may prohibit the carrying on of any business or destroy the right of work of any employee at his discretion, but he may also exempt whom he pleases from the operation of the act.

Paragraph A, section 4, reads: "The minister may from time to time, by order, designate any business or any description or class of any business as a business or a description or class thereof to which the act applies, and to except from any business or any description or class thereof any business so designated any specified class or subclass of any business or any class or subclass of persons engaged or employed therein."

Another paragraph confers on the minister power to specify any goods, wares, merchandise, etc., which may not be sold or offered for sale. His power of interference in the conduct of business will be almost unlimited. Fine or imprisonment is to be imposed for any contravention of the act. A business or occupation license may be suspended for as long a time as the minister decides and there is no right of appeal provided. He can refuse any application for a business license. This would give him power to prohibit avowed political opponents from doing business.

Legislation of this kind should not be tolerated in a democratic community. It is opposed to all democratic principles and traditions and should be fought to the last ditch by the employers and employes of the prov-ince. It proposes to impose an autocracy over individual enterprise that would be as intolerable as anything to be found in Germany or Italy today.

---

27 GOVERNMENT CONTROL OF THE PRESS?

Edmonton Bulletin
October 1, 1937

Including penalties for contravention of the act, a bill to ensure publication of news and information in newspapers agreeable to government was introduced in the Alberta legislature yesterday by Hon. Solon Low, provincial treasurer. The chairman of the board constituted by the Alberta Social Credit Act is given authority to enforce publication of any statement furnished by him affecting the objects of any government policies, the means being taken or intended to attain such objects and difficulties encountered in achieving such objects.

Every proprietor, editor, publisher or manager of any newspaper, if called upon by the board chairman in writing, must disclose every source of information contained in any statement in the newspaper, the bill declares.

The names, addresses and occupations of all persons by whom such information was furnished to the newspaper may be demanded as well as the identity of any writer of any editorial, article or news item.

The bill provides that every statement published in compliance with the act at the request of the board chairman shall be privileged and not subject to the Libel and Slander Act. No action, the bill says, may be maintained by any persons in respect to the authorized statement or subsequent publication.

In case the proprietor, editor, publisher or manager of a newspaper is guilty of any contravention of the act, the bill says the lieutenant-governor in council may upon the board chairman's recommendation, prohibit publication of the newspaper for definite time or until further order; prohibit publication or anything written by any person specified in the order or prohibit publication of any information emanating from any person or source specified.

The bill also provides every person who contravenes the act or who makes any default shall be liable to a penalty of $500; any person who contravenes any order-in-council with respect to suspension of publication or permits anyone writing who has been barred or accepts information from a barred source is subject to a penalty of $1,000.

The bill is to come into force when assented to by the lieutenant-governor.

---

28   THE GAG

Calgary Herald
October 1, 1937

For centuries it has been the unquestioned right of every British subject to speak, write or print statements or opinions on any subject without let or hindrance from his government or his neighbor. The natural and necessary check upon that right—and the only one—is that he must answer to the courts for any proved abuse of it. He may not utter slander, sedition or blasphemy without facing the judgment of a jury of his fellow citizens and the punishment of a British court.

That is freedom of speech under Anglo-Saxon law, and it is the only freedom of speech that any newspaper enjoys. Freedom of the press in British countries is no special thing, but merely the freedom of the publisher to say what any one of his fellow citizens may say in words, in writing, or in print. And under the terms of the Aberhart government's new press law that freedom would cease to exist.

For this law provides that without a hearing in court the government may, on the recommendation of one of its employees, prohibit a newspaper from publishing or a writer from getting his articles printed or a private citizen from obtaining publication of any information he may possess, no matter how vitally important that information may be to the public or to himself.

This may not be press censorship in the familiar sense of the term; but it is aimed at something worse—press control. It is a weapon cunningly designed for the extinction of responsible journalism in this province. It goes still further than that.

This law proposes not only to crush any newspaper which publishes what it knows to be the truth about the conduct of government and expenditure of public funds in Alberta, but also to compel all newspapers to publish at their own expense and regardless of whether it is true or false, a flood of government propaganda. The government plans to confiscate newspaper space without paying for it, and make whatever use of it will serve best its own ends. It could just as honestly seize a flat in an apartment house and convert it into a liquor store without paying rent.

And further still, this law provides that no one has any protection from libel or slander that may be contained in the government propaganda thus published. It proposes that the government should be able to compel a newspaper to publish anything, however libellous or damaging, about private individuals or concerns without these latter being able to protect themselves in the court, or obtain redress. This is a freedom of speech such as no British newspaper has ever enjoyed in the whole history of the press.

These things come as the climax of a long campaign in which Mr. Aberhart and his colleagues have sought to brand as rogues and liars any publications which openly criticized them. They have never once in the course of that campaign had the courage to take their grievances into court and seek the legal protection which would have been theirs for the asking if they had really been wronged. Having failed to rebut frank statements regarding themselves and their policies, they are now bringing in a measure that they hope can be used to prevent the public from reading any statements about the government which are not concocted by its own propaganda bureau.

Characteristically, they would rather try to muzzle their critics than answer them.

---

29   THE PRESS BILL

Albertan
October 4, 1937

The bill "To Ensure the Publication of Accurate News and Information", now before the legislature, and likely to be passed today, ends a right and a freedom in Alberta which have been considered a part of the British Empire for more than two hundred years.

"The Freedom of the Press" is only a phrase which can be, and frequently is, misconstrued, misunderstood, and underestimated. It is a group of five words representing not just the freedom of the individual under the British Flag. It represents the right to think freely and to give expression to the thoughts of free men and women by whatever means they may desire.

There are two sides to every story, and in the case of the Alberta government it is true to say that they have been abused and criticized by newspapers, almost beyond endurance.

There are several reasons for this. The first is that one of the penalties of public service is criticism, and, in the eyes of the public servant at least, some misrepresentation. That is inevitable in our system of democratic government, and it is one of the values of the system.

Governments have to accept it in a democracy whether they like it or not. It is a vital part of democracy, and when any government gives an indication of departing from that democratic freedom that government is inevitably moving toward dictatorship and autocracy, even if the government is innocent of intention in that regard.

Another and perhaps a major reason for the strenuous campaign against the present Alberta government, is that this government represents reform; it stands for changes in the economic system. And automatically that type of government will bring against it, not only the forces of reaction; but the forces of habit; the natural resistance to rapid change which is inherent in the human being. The Albertan said a few days ago that humanity in the mass, moves slowly and methodically toward new goals. It moves by process of evolution and the spread of education. The slowness of humanity has irritated many a reformer and caused him to try force, but the force only brought on chaos, many times bloodshed and violent death, and in the end his effort set back the clock of progress.

And so the Alberta government, as it accepted its task to change some of our system, and joined forces with the big money interests, had to expect criticism, and in its view, misrepresentation. The Albertan will say that the criticism has been more violent and more abusive and more unfair than perhaps has ever been levelled at any government in the history of the country, but the Albertan will suggest also that the best policy of the government would have been to show tolerance and patience, and not give way to anger.

Laws against freedom of speech or expression are a first move to end democracy. Closing of the courts; curbing the press in any way are sure indications of a trend. And there is nothing in civilization which can become so autocratic, so terrible, as a government agency set up in supreme control over courts and press.

To see this coming in the province of Alberta would be like a bad dream; grotesque, fantastic.

Alberta, where freedom and romance are a part of the air we breathe; a part of the open range country; the rolling hills and the sweep of wheat fields—surely it could not be in Alberta that any government would begin to limit freedom.

This government must stand for progress, and limiting freedom can not be a part of that. It must prove its case without resort to any force. When that is done it need not fear criticism of any kind, and the government can rest firmly in the belief also that the people themselves, will eventually take care of the unfair, the violent and the vicious.

Newspapers sell news, and opinions. That is their business. The opinions are not accepted by the people any more as gospel. Editorial pages do not convince in this generation, but if they stimulate thought they serve a purpose. If the news is false, untrue, or colored the people have a happy faculty of discovering the poison.

A newspaper which sells false news will eventually come to the end of the trail, just as surely as any merchant who sells bad goods.

The freedom of the press entails also the freedom of readers to judge the press, and any government can safely leave that freedom as it is.

30 ASSENT WITHHELD

Edmonton Journal
October 5, 1937

Royal assent to the new Alberta Credit Regulation act, the Taxation of Banks act, and the Accurate News and Information act, was being withheld at 3:00 p.m. Tuesday, pending instructions from the governor-general-in-council to Hon. J.C. Bowen, lieutenant-governor of Alberta.

His honor notified Robert Andison, clerk of the legislative assembly, just before the house convened at 3:00 p.m. of reasons for withholding consent.

Premier Aberhart adjourned the house for one hour and immediately summoned the Social Credit party in a caucus to which G.F. Powell, Major Douglas' representative, and G. MacLachlan, chairman of the Social Credit board, also were called.

At 3:30 p.m. there still was no indication of what would happen when the house sat again at 4:00 p.m. after the one hour adjournment.

31 DON'T RAISE THAT ISSUE

Edmonton Bulletin
October 6, 1937

Is another dangerous controversy to be started in the already surcharged political atmosphere of Alberta? The action of His Honor the Lieutenant Governor in withholding his assent to acts regularly passed by the provincial legislature, until this legislation has been considered by the Dominion Government, is a strange and alarming departure from custom. In certain circumstances the Dominion has, and has exercised, the power to disallow provincial legislation. But in so doing the federal authority acts on its own motion and its own responsibility, in defence of its own rights or those of other provinces, and without suggestion from the Lieutenant Governor of the enacting province. It is quite a different matter that this official should invoke interference, and do so in respect to legislation which has not been completely enacted. It is doubtful if there is precedent for such a course and if so it has not been recent and the practice has never been common.

The question of the justice, wisdom and expediency of the acts in question is now in danger of being pushed aside for a new issue; that of the right of the Lieutenant Governor to make such a recommendation and the right of the federal Government to pass judgment on legislation which has not yet been given the form of law.

The reaction from a controversy of that kind is obviously bound to be severe; even if history did not provide proof of the mischief inherent in raising such a contentious subject. All the more severe if thrust into a political situation already tense in the extreme. The effect of the refusal to give assent for the reason stated is to shift attention from Edmonton to Ottawa, and to arouse resentment at the use of unusual and doubtful means to block the will of the legislature. The Dominion Government would be ill-advised to sanction such procedure and incur a responsibility that does not properly belong to it. It is no part of Ottawa's duty to act as advisor to the legislature of Alberta as to what laws it shall make, and it would get small thanks for gratuitously assuming that role.

The duty of a Lieutenant Governor—as of a Governor General—to accept the advice of his Premier so long as the Premier can command a majority in the legislature has been well established. This is not the time, and certainly Alberta is not the place, to re-open that issue.

32 KING WITHHOLDS COMMENT

Albertan
October 6, 1937

While he declared he had received no communication from Lieutenant-Governor J.C. Bowen of Alberta, nor had he advised that official, on reservation of assent to provincial legislature bills, Prime Minister Mackenzie King expressed no surprise tonight when advised of the developments in Edmonton.

He understood, the prime minister said, there were "one or two bills" including a practical repetition of the recently disallowed bank regulation act, on which the lieutenant-governor would seek advice from the Governor-General-in-Council, before giving his assent.

In taking that attitude, the lieutenant-governor was acting within his constitutional responsibility, the prime minster thought, but he would not discuss the specific measures involved until they had been formally placed before the government here.

Mr. Mackenzie King presided over a long cabinet council Tuesday, the regular weekly session with his ministers, but he would not indicate whether or not Alberta developments had been discussed.

"I am for freedom of the press," the prime minister said when questioned particularly on the Alberta press legislation.

"I believe in the maintenance of all fundamental liberties."

33 ABERHART TO CALL AN ELECTION?

Edmonton Bulletin
October 7, 1937

Premier Aberhart hinted last night that a general election may be called in Alberta if the federal government advises Lieutenant-Governor J.C. Bowen not to sign three bills passed at the recent special session of the Alberta legislature, but reserved by the Lieutenant-Governor "at the pleasure of the Governor-General."

In an address before 700 people [at Milk River] he told of events during the last hour and half before the legislature was prorogued Tuesday, October 5.

"The Lieutenant-Governor called me in at two minutes to 3 p.m.," Mr. Aberhart said, "with no intimation of such a thing before, to tell me he must refer three bills. There has never been a precedent for such action in Alberta. The Lieutenant-Governor is supposed to take the advice of the premier.

"Now if Ottawa says, 'No' I have nothing more to say. You must do the talking."

Earlier in his address the premier said:

"If I don't get the will of the people I may have to call an election."

"My appeal to you is to express yourself kindly and definitely," he said as he concluded his address.

Mr. Aberhart said the new Bank Act, one of the measures referred to the federal government, was misunderstood. The provincial government, he declared, had no wish to interfere with banks, but they must not have the full power to monetize credit.

Referring to the act "to ensure the publication of accurate news and information," another of the bills on which the leiutenant-governor reserved his signature, the premier said, was mainly one of obtaining the privilege of correcting wrongs. The government did not intend to interfere with a free press.

Provincial Treasurer, Solon Low, accompanying the premier on his speaking tour through southern Alberta this week, also defended the government's record.

"We are not on the run," he said. "Today we stand in a better position than for many months." He thought the proposed $2,000,000 tax on banks was not so high. The smelter in Trail, B.C., alone paid $2,000,000 tax.

"We are thwarted by having this bank taxation act—clearly intra-vires—set aside by the lieutenant-governor," the provincial secretary declared, "if we haven't the right to tax, this province has no control over property and civil rights.

"It may look like we have been stopped but we have a set result and we are going to accomplish it. We can't divulge everything."

34 PRESS GAG OPPOSED

Calgary Herald
October 12, 1937

The Alberta division of the Canadian Weekly Newspapers' Association has put itself formally on record as being utterly opposed to legislation seeking to restrict the liberty of the press. A strongly worded resolution to that effect was adopted at the annual convention in Edmonton last week.

No government in the history of this or any other province has been accorded so much free space as the newspapers of Alberta, daily and weekly, have given the "social credit" administration. But on the other hand no government in this country has won so little editorial commendation and the reason is plain. Its policies and objectives when not chaotic are destructive.

As a result of this inevitable failure to attract press support, the "social credit" heads, even before they entered office, did not hesi-

tate to apply the obnoxious principle of boycott to their newspaper opponents. Both
publicly and privately, the spirit of intolerance to criticism was voiced. Weeklies as well
as dailies have known what it is to be threatened with loss of circulation and advertising
patronage unless they changed, or at least
modified, their editorial attitude. But there
has only been one case in the province of a
newspaper swinging over from criticism to
support of "social credit" since the election of
1935.

"Social credit" boycotting methods have
not been dropped. It is only a few weeks since
the government "group" at Ardmore threatened the Bonnyville Nouvelle with loss of
business unless it changed its editorial policy.
The communication received the defiance it
deserved.

Adverse press opinion has been fully
justified by the failure of the government to
make good any of the promises on which it
was elected. It was recognized early in the
1935 campaign, by practically every Alberta
newspaper, that a huge hoax was being
perpetrated on the electors. And last March,
Mr. Aberhart finally threw up his hands and
in a burst of frankness acknowledged he had
no plan. Since then the government has been
directed from London.

Having failed to attract favorable press
opinion, the government, under the inspira-
tion of Major Douglas, hit on the expedient of
muzzling the newspapers and making them
publish propaganda in its favor free of
charge. This un-British plan has been balked
by the refusal of the Lieutenant-Governor to
sign the press gag bill, and the Alberta press is
still free to express its views without dictation
from Aberhart and his expensive "social
credit" board.

35 ABERHART ASKS FOR COURT RULING

Edmonton Journal
October 18, 1937

Reference to the courts of the question of the
federal rights of disallowance of provincial
legislation is suggested in a letter from Premier Aberhart to Premier King, the text of
which was released by the former here

Monday.

Dealing with the three bills which Hon.
J.C. Bowen, lieutenant-governor, referred to
Ottawa for consideration, royal assent being
reserved to the governor-general, Premier
Aberhart suggests that the press bill "might
well be referred to the courts."

The bank taxation and credit regulations
bills "can only be properly dealt with by a
test case," says Mr. Aberhart's letter.

When the special session of the Alberta
house was prorogued on October 5, the three
bills on which the lieutenant-governor reserved for the "signification of his excellency
the governor-general's pleasure thereon"
were: An act to ensure the publication of accurate news and information; an act respecting the taxation of banks; an act to amend
and consolidate the Credit of Alberta Regulation act, commonly known as the bank licensing act.

Following the session, acting-Premier
Fallow communicated with Premier King
asking whether the dominion would consider
representations from the province before
making a decision on the three acts. Premier
King replied that a decision would be withheld until representations were made and
asked that a submission be forwarded as early
as possible.

Last Wednesday night, the letter from Premier Aberhart giving the province's stand in
the matter was forwarded to Premier King.
Release was withheld here to make certain
that sufficient time had elapsed for the federal
premier to receive it.

Premier Aberhart's letter, referring to the
question of disallowance, recalls that the
province already has contended that the dominion does not hold such a right.

"We should respectfully suggest that to
maintain a harmonious relationship between
the provincial and federal governments, that
this important question should be definitely
settled by the courts," says Mr. Aberhart.

The province contends, according to the
letter, that its legislation "is law and should
remain law until declared ultra vires by the
courts."

"Therefore, we urge that the question
might well be referred to the courts for determination," says Mr. Aberhart.

Referring to the press bill, the Alberta premier says that "should there be any doubt as

to the constitutional validity of the press bill, we have no objection to having it referred to the courts along with the question of disallowance."

Dealing with the two banking bills, Mr. Aberhart says these are in a different category to the other questions.

"The question involved is one more of fact than of law and consequently it would be necessary to submit evidence to the courts in order to enable them to give a proper decision," says the Alberta premier.

36   CREDIT MUST BE CONTROLLED

Edmonton Bulletin
October 25, 1937

It is evident that people are realizing more and more that the enemies of democracy, confederation and the unity of the British Empire are not members of the Social Credit government, but those who oppose the adjustment "of our economic and social structure to meet the requirement of the people." Hon Ernest C. Manning, minister of trade and industry and provincial secretary declared here Sunday evening in an address before the Edmonton Prophetic Bible Conference at the Strand theatre.

He added that it was futile to talk of controlling the credit of the people while the present system held sway.

"In these days," he said, "when the province seems to be suffering from an epidemic of organizations whose chief function seems to be to vie with each other to see which can throw the most mud, be the most scathing in destructive criticism and spread the most anti-government propaganda, it is encouraging to know that the vast majority are quite able to detect the real motive and the political aspirations behind the disgraceful display of cheap political propaganda.

"There always have been and always will be those who are glad to criticize, abuse and misrepresent, even though they themselves seldom, if ever, lift a hand in an honest endeavor to better the conditions of their fellow man.

"May I repeat what I said at Saskatoon that we are not a bunch of wild American Indians running around trying to kick holes in the Canadian constitution.

"We are a group of common, ordinary, everyday, peace-loving, law-abiding British subjects, with every bit as much love for and loyalty to our King, our country and our flag as anyone in Canada.

"We are not secessionists, nor anti-Confederationists. We believe in the liberty and freedom that characterizes the British Empire and this Dominion through the strength of Confederation.

"But we are sufficiently awake to what is going on in the world to realize that the cords of loyalty and confederation will be more and more severely strained unless our present financial and economic structure is adjusted.

"Our fight, therefore, is to preserve democracy, not to destroy it.

"It is evident that people are realizing more and more that the great enemies of democracy and confederation and the unity of our great Empire, is not the Alberta Social Credit government, but those who oppose adjustment of our economic and social structure to meet the requirements of our people.

"I might summarize as threefold, the attitude of the thinking citizens of this province.

"In the first place, there is a growing disgust toward those who are lending themselves to the cheap mudslinging type of criticism abroad in Alberta today.

"In the second place, there is a growing conviction that the major issue for which we are fighting is fundamental to all permanent economic and social security and freedom, namely the control of credit.

"In the third place, there is a growing determination to see that the government be given a fair opportunity to accomplish that which we have been given a mandate to carry out."

Mr. Manning stressed the necessity of the government gaining control of its credit as this was the first step in a broader program of rehabilitation and introduction of the new social and economic era, toward which the Alberta government of the day was working and moving.

He announced that on Wednesday, Hon. Solon E. Low and Floyd M. Baker, member for Clover Bar would speak at Ardrossan hall and that next Saturday, at New Sarepta at 8 p.m., Mr. Baker and probably two other M.L.A.'s would speak.

37 FEDERAL CABINET FAVOURS COURT RULING

Edmonton Journal
November 2, 1937

The dominion government announced Tuesday night it would recommend reference to the supreme court of Canada of three contentious bills passed by the Alberta legislature at its October special session. The court will be asked to rule on their constitutionality.

The bills upon which the court would be asked to rule as to their validity are:

1. An act respecting the taxation of banks.
2. An act to consolidate and amend the Credit of Alberta Regulation act.
3. An act to ensure the publication of accurate news and information.

Text of the reference to the supreme court has been drafted by dominion officials and this, with copies of the three measures, would be forwarded to proper officers of the tribunal.

Until the supreme court gives its decision, royal assent would be held in abeyance leaving the measures without legal force.

Given third readings at the special session of the Alberta legislature which opened Sept. 24, these three bills were reserved for the signification of the pleasure of his excellency, the governor-general thereon, at a sensational sitting on Oct. 5 when the house was prorogued by the lieutenant-governor.

When Premier Aberhart learned from his honor just before prorogation that royal assent on the three bills in question would be referred to Ottawa the house was adjourned for an hour during which Social Credit members were in caucus.

When the house reassembled, his honor gave formal assent to eight bills passed at the session while it was announced that the three others were being referred to Ottawa for final disposal.

Later official copies of the acts passed at the special session were forwarded to Ottawa by Robert Andison, clerk of the legislative assembly.

Some days later, Hon. W.A. Fallow, then acting premier in the absence of Premier Aberhart who was in the southern part of the province, asked Premier King if the dominion would hear representations from the province concerning the three bills before they were disposed of by the federal authorities. Mr. King replied at once acceding to the request but asked that a written submission should be forwarded as soon as possible.

The province's submission was mailed to Ottawa on Oct. 13 and released in Edmonton by Premier Aberhart Oct. 18 for publication.

The province contended, according to the letter to Premier King, that the banking and regulation of credit (bank licensing) acts should be left to be settled by test actions in the courts. It suggested that it "might be well to refer any question as to the constitutional validity of the press act to the courts."

38 LEGAL ARRAY SET FOR HEARING

Edmonton Journal
January 5, 1938

Dry, abstruse submissions of law upon which next week's arguments before the supreme court regarding the Alberta legislation will be based are the whole nature of the factums exchanged Wednesday. One side thus knows what the other one will contend, and will be prepared to answer.

The submissions are in the usual form consisting of factual statements concerning the dominion government's exercise of the prerogative of disallowance of some acts and the act of the lieutenant-governor in reserving his assent to other acts pending "signification of his excellency's pleasure."

In plain language, this "signification" business means that Hon. J.C. Bowen, lieutenant-governor, simply held back his assent until he got advice from Ottawa as to whether or not he should give it. And he is still waiting to hear.

The Alberta government having questioned the propriety of any such process, the dominion government has referred the whole question to the courts. The references covered the whole field of constitutional conflict over the statutes in question.

There will be before the court what commonly is called a "distinguished array" of counsel with silken robes and fine facilities of argument for or against or on both sides.

Very big lawyers, retained by government's get as high as $500 a day. Assistants get less but $50 is the very minimum. Lawyers, regularly employed by governments, receive no extra remuneration for their work save expenses.

The legal costs of the coming argument will probably mount to $3,000 a day. The calculation is that, on the question of disallowance, the argument will take about two days on the specific acts; seven or eight more may be consumed but at the latest argument is expected to be over by Jan. 21.

Judgments in the supreme court are never delivered summarily in a case like this; the judges have a conference room where after the conclusion of a case they get together and confer.

If they agree it is the custom to delegate one judge to write the reasons for judgment. If they disagree then majority and minority conclusions are written. In the supreme court, here, judgments never are simply handed down—filed with the registrar. They always are delivered in open court on a day which is announced. Only the general result is then made known. In these references to each question, it will be announced whether the answer is "yes" or "no".

Full texts of the "reasons" are immediately available for counsel and the press and with the greatest courtesy.

The arguments next week will probably be as dry as are the factums today. They always are. It is most improbable that throughout, the name of Mr. Aberhart or Mr. Mackenzie King or any other public man will be mentioned. "Highlights" if any will be few.

It will simply be a long discussion, pro and con, as to whether disallowance is or is not a federal prerogative and whether this statute or that is "ultra vires" of the legislation or "within its legislative competence."

There is no analogy whatever between an appeal in the supreme court on a cold question of law and a sparkling jury case on a question of fact. On the opening day the judges come in wearing brilliant red gowns trimmed with ermine. On the other days black silk suffices.

Judgments will be expected comparatively early, but that will depend upon how the cases develop. References of the sort are decided as soon as possible but great care is taken in deciding the nature and the verbiage of pronouncement. Inevitably one side or other will take it to the privy council.

---

39 JUDGES RESERVE DECISION

Edmonton Bulletin
January 11, 1938

Six judges of the Supreme Court took under consideration Monday federal power to disallow provincial legislation and the power of lieutenant-governors to reserve assent for signification of the governor-general's pleasure.

At the end of a full day in court, Chief Justice Sir Lyman Duff signified the judges would reserve decision on the constitutional reference which arose from Alberta protests over use of the powers of disallowance and reservation during the last six months.

The court today will consider constitutionality of three Alberta bills to which Lieutenant-Governor John Bowen reserved assent in September but there was no indication last night which would be considered first. They deal with bank taxation, control of credit institutions and newspaper regulation.

Disallowance has been exercised more than 100 times since the British North America act was passed in 1867, and the present Canadian system of government came into operation. The last time provincial legislation was vetoed apart from Alberta statutes in August was 1924.

Aimé Geoffrion, chief counsel for the Dominion, contended powers of disallowance and reservation were embodied in the British North America act and remain today, unimpaired and unlimited.

For Alberta, O.M. Biggar argued it was impossible to reconcile some constitutional practices with wording of the B.N.A. act and cited court decisions purporting to show terminology of the act must be changed to cover constitutional evolutions.

The Alberta counsel claimed the Dominion's power to disallow provincial statutes had lapsed because the 1935 Imperial conference denied to the parliament of Great Britain the power to veto Dominion statutes. He showed the wording of the B.N.A. Act remained the same today, embodying Imperial disallowance, even in the face of the imperial conference decision. This, he claimed, was an example of constitutional evolution taking priority over the wording of a statute.

Replying for the Dominion, Mr. Geoffrion contended the Imperial power of disallowance remained just as it was before 1926, the only effect of the Imperial conference being the British government agreed not to exercise it. In any event, growth of Canada into a self-governing, autonomous nation had no bearing on the relationship between Dominion and provinces.

40 DISALLOWANCE ACTS DISCUSSED

Edmonton Bulletin
February 5, 1938

Rt. Hon. Ernest Lapointe, minister of justice, continued the address debate in the House of Commons Friday. He dealt with disallowance and reservation of Alberta enactments and the supreme court of Canada reference.

The justice minister upheld the practice of referring to the supreme court, federal or provincial legislation of which there were constitutional doubts. That, he said, was one of the reasons for establishing the court.

All three of the disallowed Alberta statutes, including the bank-license law, contained provisions to stop court action in the province, Mr. Lapointe said. The bank bill was a direct invasion of the federal legislative field and ran contrary to Dominion enactments on banking.

Premier Aberhart "refused bluntly" to suspend application of the three bills while they were referred to the court, Mr. Lapointe said. After that, there was no course open to the Dominion government but to veto the three laws.

Rt. Hon. R.B. Bennett, Conservative leader, had alleged discrimination against Alberta because the Ontario power contracts legislation had not been disallowed. Mr. Bennett, being a great authority, all the Social Credit and C.C.F. members had followed him and made the same charge.

It was easy to show the distinction between the Ontario statute and those of Alberta. No two statutes disallowed or considered for disallowance were the same.

It had become a rule that a law should not be disallowed merely because it was ultra vires. The courts could deal with it. It should not be disallowed unless it interfered with some policy or legislation of the Dominion. It was for the electors of Ontario to deal with questions of injustice or unfairness in Ontario legislation.

"And we were right in our decision on the Ontario statute," said Mr. Lapointe. "Since then it has been successfully challenged in the courts and a judgment against it obtained. The matter has now been settled to the satisfaction of all the parties concerned."

Turning again to the Alberta bank license bill, Mr. Lapointe claimed it was a clear invasion of the federal legislative field. It was a deliberate attempt to substitute provincial banking laws for federal laws.

Mr. Lapointe reiterated that Canada should have the power to amend its own constitution.

"We are the only Dominion in the British Empire which has not this power," he said. "We are the only federal country in the world which has not the power in some form."

Those who suggested there was something sacred and unchangeable in a constitution were mistaken. One generation had no right to bind a future generation by imposing on it an unchangeable constitution.

The Dominion government will decide in the next few weeks whether it will disallow the Quebec padlock law, it was announced by Mr. Lapointe.

Three or four days ago a petition for disallowance was received by the government, the minister of justice declared, which must be considered before the end of March, the limit of the year in which the Dominion may veto the provincial anti-Communist law.

Facing members of the house who had urged disallowance of the Quebec padlock law, Mr. Lapointe said it would surprise them to know he received only three or four days ago a petition to veto it. There had been many telegrams and resolutions but only one official and regular petition upon which he must act.

Following him in the address debate, Hon. C.H. Cahan, secretary of state in the Bennett administration, asked if it would not be wise to wait another year before seeking legal power to establish unemployment insurance.

At the same time, Mr. Cahan suggested the Dominion, in addition to seeking control over unemployment insurance, should include legislative authority over hours of employment, minimum wages and the right to arbitrate and adjust labor disputes. These are collateral measures to an unemployment insurance scheme and, if the Dominion did not control them, they might endanger the effectiveness of the insurance plan.

---

41 SUPREME COURT OF CANADA RULING

Edmonton Journal
March 4, 1938

Supreme court of Canada Friday ruled invalid three Alberta bills dealing with credit regulation, bank taxes and newspapers, and upheld the federal government's power of disallowance of provincial legislation and the right of a lieutenant-governor to reserve assent on provincial legislation.

In addition, Chief Justice Duff found against the Alberta Social Credit act, considered to be the cornerstone of the Alberta Social Credit government's design.

In a series of judgments, the court:

1. Held to be unconstitutional an act to amend and consolidate the Credit of Alberta Regulation act;

2. Held to be unconstitutional the Taxation of Banks act;

3. Held to be unconstitutional the act "to ensure the publication of accurate news and information";

4. Ruled the dominion had power to disallow provincial enactments without restriction;

5. Ruled lieutenant-governors had power to reserve their assent from provincial legislation subject only to any instructions from the governor-general.

On every subject, the court ruled against the submissions of the provincial government as outlined at the hearing held here from Jan. 10 to Jan. 17, and accepted the arguments of the dominion on every point.

Each of the six judges arrived at the same decision and the court was unanimous in the judgments. Some of the judges, however, arrived at the decisions by different reasoning.

The main judgment of the court was written by Chief Justice Sir Lyman Duff and Mr. Justice Davis, Mr. Justice Cannon and Kerwin wrote separate judgments arriving at the same decisions, Mr. Justice Crocket agreeing with the latter judgment, Mr. Justice Hudson wrote a separate judgment.

Going outside the terms of the reference, Chief Justice Duff passed an opinion on the Alberta Social Credit act, which he found to be outside the legal jurisdiction of the province.

This opinion was considered one of the most important of all because it threw doubt on the whole plan of the Aberhart government to institute a Social Credit financial scheme in Alberta.

The chief justice, when dealing with the three bills, found it necessary to examine "the general scheme and history of the (Social Credit) legislation" of Alberta. Although the Social Credit act was not involved in the reference, he found it necessary to examine it. His decision was that it transgressed the legal powers of the province as defined in the British North America act.

---

42 COURT DECISIONS DISAPPOINT PREMIER

Edmonton Journal
March 4, 1938

Premier Aberhart expressed his disappointment Friday over the supreme court of Canada decisions against three Alberta bills and against provincial claims in disallowance and reservation of assent.

Just what step might be taken in consequence of the court rulings, the premier was not prepared to say.

"Naturally I am disappointed over the decisions," said the premier." "I would not care to make any comment, however, until I have had an opportunity to give more consideration to the situation and have more information on the judgments."

While the Ottawa court decisions were disappointing, Premier Aberhart said the government will carry on "business as usual" and await detailed information on the supreme court rulings.

The premier said there was no suggestion as to adjourning the house, in view of the decisions. Business would be proceeded with as intended, he said.

A cabinet meeting was held on Friday, but the Ottawa judgments were not considered in view of the fact that full information was not yet at hand, said the premier.

Private Social Credit members discussed the judgments in small groups, but made no comment for publication. There seemed to be a general view that in view of the federal disallowance powers being upheld, it was practically useless in trying to pass Social Credit legislation.

Opinions of the supreme court of Canada were received by G.L. MacLachlan, Social Credit, Coronation, and chairman of the Social Credit board, as "a keen disappointment."

"They also will be a keen disappointment to the poverty stricken people of this province," he said. "I will reserve further comment on the decisions until I know texts of the judgments."

Hon. Solon Low, provincial treasurer, voiced disappointment over the throwing out of the bank taxation bill, under which the province hoped to tax banks $2,000,000 annually.

"While I would want to see the full text of the judgment before passing any definite opinions, it seems to me that when such a bill as the one dealing with bank taxation is thrown out, one might question whether we can tax anything under our property and civil rights," Mr. Low observed.

"Will it affect the budget?" Mr. Low was asked.

"Yes," he replied. "We had expected that the bank taxation bill would offset the deficit which we have budgeted for in the next fiscal year."

Mr. Low, it is recalled, in delivering his budget speech last Friday, mentioned the bank taxation as possibly offsetting the overall estimated deficit of $1,567,000 for the 1938-39 fiscal year.

Decisions of the supreme court are expected to be discussed at a cabinet meeting Friday.

In all likelihood, the situation also will be talked over by the Social Crediters at a caucus during the day.

Judging by comment, Friday, it is unlikely that any new legislation will be introduced at the present session of the house as a substitute for the acts which have been thrown out by the supreme court of Canada.

Practically all the major legislation for the present session has been brought down, with the exception of the debt adjustment act, securities taxation bill and amendments to the income tax act. Unless some new policy is decided upon by the S.C. caucus, it seems unlikely that there will be any other major bills.

43 THE COURT'S DECISION

Albertan
March 5, 1938

Judgments handed down by the Supreme Court of Canada yesterday on Alberta's Social Credit legislation were sweeping and complete.

The decision of the highest Canadian court was unanimous and that unanimity was only emphasized by the fact that the judges arrived at the same decision by different routes.

In addition, the Chief Justice stepped aside in his findings to review the background of Social Credit legislation in Alberta, and he indicated clearly enough his opinion that the whole scheme was illegal and unconstitutional.

The judgments do several things. Definitely enough they mark the end of another chapter in what Major Douglas once called "The Alberta Experiment," and it will be in the minds of many Alberta people that we are approaching the last chapter and the last phase of an attempt by one province to change the economic system.

The approach to our economic problems—and the problems certainly exist—must obviously be more powerful than the power that can be generated in one provincial legislature. The attack must come from a Canada-wide belief in the need for a change and a Canada-wide conception of the right road to follow.

One province cannot touch the economic set-up of Canada. The judgments, if they are final, make that clear enough and it would only be pathetic folly for any section of the people of Alberta to go on believing that one province has the power to regulate banking or credit or to superimpose a new credit system on the old.

The decisions indicate clearly enough the narrow field within which any province can legislate. And after one attempts to legislate the Lieutenant-Governor can withhold consent while bills are referred to the Dominion.

The majority of the people of Alberta will be wondering today what the next step will be. The Government's answer may be the Privy Council, but the fact might as well be faced that an appeal to the Privy Council can hold small chance of any substantial change in the findings. The unanimous and definite verdict of the Canadian Supreme Court might be held unsound by the Privy Council, but that seems doubtful. And so there is only a slim hope there for the government at Edmonton.

In the midst of this new development it is too early to predict the eventual outcome as it will affect the government and the people of Alberta, and it is not time yet to review the past. The past is still too closely related to the present.

Shortly, however, there must come a clearer picture. The immediate future must be made more definite and it is the duty of the government to provide the definite view.

Business in Alberta requires stability and security and there must be a limit to experimental legislation under which credit dies.

---

44 ALBERTA PAPERS GIVEN PULITZER PRIZES

Edmonton Journal
May 2, 1938

Newspapers of Alberta Tuesday accepted an unprecedented tribute from the Pulitzer prize committee for their "struggle to preserve the freedom of the press" in the Canadian province.

The committee made a double break with custom for the first time in its 21 years' history by awarding a bronze plaque to *Edmonton Journal* and engraved certificates to five other Alberta dailies and 90 weekly newspapers.

Never before had the committee looked beyond the borders of the United States to make an award, and never before had a special award been made.

The plaque went to *Edmonton Journal* "for its leadership in the defence of the freedom of the press in the province of Alberta," and to the other papers for their co-operation in the fight against the restrictive legislation passed by the Social Credit government.

Accepting the awards in behalf of the newspapers of the province, John M. Imrie, vice-president and managing director of *Edmonton Journal*, said in the course of a moving address: "The struggle was for much more than a free press. It was for democracy itself." Mr. Imrie emphasized that government control of the press was "an indispensable instrument of dictatorship."

The measure against which the newspapers fought was the Alberta press act of October, 1937, which would have required newspapers to reveal the sources of their information and also to print statements handed out by the government.

The five dailies receiving engraved certificates are: the *Herald* and *Albertan,* Calgary; the *Bulletin,* Edmonton; the *Herald,* Lethbridge; and the *News,* Medicine Hat.

Dean Carl W. Ackerman of the Columbia School of Journalism said after the awards were announced that the special tribute to the Alberta newspapers "undoubtedly is the greatest thing in the history of the Pulitzer committee."

In presenting Mr. Imrie, who sat among the score at the head table, to the gathering of 500 at the silver anniversary dinner of the Columbia school of journalism, Dean Ackerman said the decision of the supreme court of Canada finding the Alberta press act unconstitutional was "one of the greatest legal decisions of this period of world change."

He recalled that the presiding justice of the supreme court had said: "The freedom of the press is essential to public opinion and public discussion, which in turn are necessary to parliamentary government." Dean Ackerman said that under the leadership of Mr. Imrie, the newspapers of Alberta had "successfully fought for and maintained the free press throughout the whole of Canada."

Mr. Imrie, in concluding his address of thanks for the awards rededicated the press of Alberta to "continue with unabated vigor, without equivocation or surrender, the struggle to preserve inviolate in Alberta those fundamentals of liberty and freedom that are the common and glorious heritage of your people and mine."

Mr. Imrie said he was deeply grateful "for the recognition thus given to the struggle of the Alberta newspapers to preserve the freedom of the press within that province."

It was the very essence of democracy, Mr. Imrie said, that the people should have an opportunity to know and freedom to discuss the activities and policies of their government. The formation of intelligent public opinion was "the motivating force and the effective safeguard of true democracy."

Guide to Journals

Alberta Social Credit Chronicle

Founded in Calgary in July 1934 as a publicity medium for the Social Credit movement under editor Charles Underwood. It appeared to preach to the already converted with doctrinaire articles and columns, as, for example, "Through a Social Credit Window, by Mac". It was supported by subscription and advertising revenue, though the editor refused to publish "any liquor or crude medicinal advertising that may be high priced but entirely detrimental to the clean[n]ess of the paper." Merged with the *Albertan* as a Saturday supplement in January 1936. The paper ceased publication on August 13, 1938.

[Calgary] Albertan

Founded in 1902, and generally a supporter of the Liberal party under various publishers. Subsidized by the *Calgary Herald* from 1932 to 1936 to keep it out of the evening field, excepting seven months of 1934, when it appeared as an evening publication. In January 1936, an agreement for sale was arranged with Social Credit leaders, whereby stock was offered to the public and "*Calgary*" was dropped from the masthead. After the failure of sales efforts, the agreement lapsed in 1939, ownership reverting to Max Bell, son of the former publisher. Before 1936, the *Albertan* supported the provincial Liberals, but opened its letter columns to Social Crediters. While linked to Social Credit, editorial policy was favourable, and friendly outside press comment, when available, was extensively printed in its own columns. In 1938, an open break with Social Credit resulted from editor Peter Galbraith's criticism of the

117

press control bill, and his acceptance of unfavourable court decisions on key Social Credit legislation.

Calgary Herald

Founded in 1883 and purchased by the Southam family in 1908. Adopted and pursued a hostile editorial policy toward Social Credit under various publishers, but carried extensive news dispatches and letters to the editor relating to the movement. In addition to its editorial broadsides against Social Credit, the *Herald* carried the cartoon lampoons of Aberhart drawn by Stewart Cameron.

The newspaper also reflected strongly the farm and ranch interests in Calgary's hinterland in its extensive rural news and opposition to compulsory pasteurization of milk.

Edmonton Bulletin

Founded in 1880, and a consistent supporter of the Liberal party, especially under the early ownership of Frank Oliver, Minister of the Interior, 1905-1911. It continued to support federal and provincial Liberals in the thirties, though supporting policies of extensive government spending, at times using the Labour government of New Zealand as its model. It ceased publication in 1951.

Edmonton Journal

Founded in 1909 and purchased by the Southams in 1912. More moderate in its opposition to Social Credit than the *Calgary Herald*, but still consistently hostile to the Aberhart government. By 1944, it had swung over to the support of Premier Ernest Manning, but "diluted" its editorial approval in the years that followed.

Ottawa Citizen

Founded in 1844 as the Bytown *Packet*, later renamed the *Citizen* in 1851, and was purchased by Wilson Southam in 1897. In the twenties and thirties, its editor, Charles Bowman, promoted the Social Credit philosophy of Major Douglas, and despite doubts about Aberhart's interpretation of it, was generally sympathetic to Alberta Social Credit. The historian of the Southam press indicates, however, that the *Citizen*'s "voice was scarcely heard in the West" in this period.

Today and Tomorrow

Established in Edmonton in late 1935 as an organ of the Social Credit movement in northern Alberta. Edited by Lucien Maynard, whose advancement in Alberta cabinet positions was well publicized in its pages. Similar in format and content to the *Alberta Social Credit Chronicle* published in Calgary. It ceased publication on October 5, 1944, and was superseded by the *Canadian Social Crediter* a week later.

Winnipeg Free Press

Originally founded as the *Manitoba Free Press*, and noted for the long editorship of John W. Dafoe. Hostile to Social Credit, as was most of the press outside Alberta. In 1938, when Dafoe was appointed to the Royal Commission on Dominion-Provincial Relations, Aberhart angrily described the paper as "one of the worst yellow journals of the West ...a publication which has been constantly bitter in its hostility to this Government, and the concept of political and economic democracy to which Alberta is committed."

Bibliographic Essay

In the 1950s the Canadian Social Science Research Council funded a series of publications under the general editorship of S.D. Clark, intended to clarify the meaning of the extraordinary events surrounding the sudden rise to power of Social Credit in Alberta. Never before or since has so much scholarly talent in Canada been devoted to western Canadian development. In his contribution to the series, J.A. Irving surveyed the then unorganized written documents relating to Social Credit and conducted extensive interviews with survivors of the thirties, bringing together his conclusions into a classic study of group psychology. Political theorist, C.B. Macpherson, produced a profound study of the nature of the democratic process in Alberta, by exploring the complex interaction of political theory and practice during the United Farmer and Social Credit periods, and by speculating on the theoretical origins of Social Credit in England. The larger constitutional context of Dominion-Provincial relations which framed the unsuccessful struggle by Social Credit to implement its legislation was described in another volume by J.R. Mallory. The political background of the Social Credit movement in western Canada was described by two historians, one by L.G. Thomas on the Liberal Party period in Alberta before 1921, and the other by W.L. Morton on the role of the Progressive Party of Canada during the twenties, a party in which the United Farmers of Alberta played an important part. Other ground-breaking studies by sociologists, Jean Burnet and W.E. Mann established the rural and urban context of prairie society which sustained the Social Credit movement in power. These volumes in the "Social Credit in Alberta" series are essential companion pieces to any further study of the movement.

In 1959, Harold Schultz produced a doctoral dissertation for Duke University, which remains the only academic biography of William Aberhart. Since then, he has written a series of articles, both biographical and analytical, which do much to explain the Social Credit movement and its first Canadian leader. More recently, Aberhart's daughter, Mrs. Ola MacNutt and Professor L.P.V. Johnson of the University of Alberta have written an understandably loyal and sympathetic portrait of a man much maligned in his lifetime by hostile critics.

While the co-authors claim that Aberhart's personal papers "are most remarkable for their dearth", Aberhart's official papers are available. The Provincial Archives of Alberta now contain a wealth of material in the files used by Aberhart during his tenure. And in due course, they will also have those of his successor, Ernest Manning, thus providing present and future researchers with materials comparable to those of other Canadian public figures. Many further questions remain to be answered, but the materials are at hand.

For Further Reading

Alberta.	*The Case for Alberta.* Edmonton: King's Printer, 1938.
Barr, John J.	*The Dynasty: The Rise and Fall of Social Credit in Alberta.* Toronto: McClelland and Stewart, 1974.
Bowman, Charles.	*Ottawa Editor, the Memoirs of Charles Bowman.* Sidney (British Columbia): Gray's Publishing Ltd., 1966.
Bruce, Charles.	*News and the Southams.* Toronto: Macmillan, 1968.
Clark, S.D., ed.	Social Credit in Alberta, Its Background and Development. Toronto: University of Toronto Press, 1953-1959:-

1. Morton, W.L., *The Progressive Party in Canada.*

2. Masters, D.C., *The Winnipeg General Strike.*

3. Burnet, Jean, *Next-Year Country.*

4. Macpherson, C.B., *Democracy in Alberta.*

5. Mallory, J.R., *Social Credit and the Federal Power in Canada.*

6. Mann, W.E., *Sect, Cult and Church in Alberta.*

7. Fowke, V.C., *The National Policy and the Wheat Economy.*

8. Thomas, L.G., *The Liberal Party in Alberta: A History of Politics in the Province of Alberta, 1905-1921.*

9. Clark, S.D., *Movements of Political Protest in Canada, 1640-1840.*

10. Irving, J.A., *The Social Credit Movement in Alberta.*

Canada.	*Report of the Royal Commission on Dominion-Provincial Relations.* Ottawa: King's Printer, 1940.
Douglas, Clifford H.	*Social Credit.* 3rd ed. London: Eyre and Spottiswood, 1933.
————	*The Alberta Experiment.* London: Eyre and Spottiswood, 1937.
Finlay, John L.	*Social Credit: The English Origins.* Montreal: McGill-Queen's University Press, 1972.
Horn, Michiel.	*The Dirty Thirties: Canadians in the Great Depression.* Toronto: Copp Clark, 1972.

James, Norman. *Autobiography of a Nobody.* Toronto: Dent, 1947.

Johnson, L.P.V. and
MacNutt, Ola. *Aberhart of Alberta.* Edmonton: Institute of Applied Art, 1970.

Kesterton, W.H. *A History of Journalism in Canada* (Carleton Library, No. 36). Toronto: McClelland and Stewart, 1967.

Lipset, S.M. *Agrarian Socialism: The Cooperative Commonwealth Federation in Saskatchewan: A Study in Political Sociology.* Berkeley: University of California Press, 1950.

Neatby, L.B. *The Politics of Chaos: Canada in the Thirties.* Toronto: Macmillan, 1972.

Saywell, John. *The Office of the Lieutenant-Governor: A Study in Canadian Government and Politics.* Toronto: University of Toronto Press, 1957.

———— "Reservation Revisited: 1937," *Canadian Journal of Economics and Political Science,* XXVII (August, 1961), 361-371.

Schultz, Harold. "Aberhart, the Organization Man," *Alberta Historical Review,* VII (Spring, 1959) 19-26.

———— "A Second Term: 1940," *Alberta Historical Review,* X (Winter, 1962) 17-26.

———— "Portrait of a Premier: William Aberhart," *Canadian Historical Review,* XLV (September, 1964), 185-211.

———— "The Social Credit Back-benchers' Revolt, 1937," *Canadian Historical Review,* XLI (March, 1960) 1-18.